Men's Chronicles: A Woman's Guide to Men Presents...

The Four Women that Men Desire

Sir Walter Jones

ISBN: 978-0-578-44417-8

Scripture references marked KJV are taken from the
King James Version of the Bible;
NLT refers to the New Living Translation.

Dedication

I would sincerely like to dedicate this book to The Founders, the Greatest Generation and the main reason why I didn't rot in jail. To my Madea, Dorothy Starnes (My mom's mother), who took me in as a teenager during my rebellious years against my parents. She never sugar coated anything, always told me the truth about myself and didn't allow me to bring girls up in her house when she wasn't there. At the time of this release, she's yet telling me what to do, in her mid-90s.

To my other living Granny who we affectionately call "Mother", Hattie B. Jones. I was always a bit scared of her because she was Chicago's famed Prophetess who was always accurate. Dad made us go over to her house for special holidays, but we couldn't be kids around her because her entire house looked like a white palace and everything you sat on was covered in plastic. Before she retired from cooking home meals, Mother made the best hoe cakes in town. She's knocking on 100 soon and I think she's in competition with her late Father who surpassed that age.

To the memory of two great spiritual fathers who have both entered eternity recently...both were from the last crop of Holiness Preachers in America. Bishop Lorenzo Kelly was not just my Pastor, he was my friend. We literally did everything together – ran the streets, read books, watched movies and cooked. He showed me so much about leadership, fatherhood and how to always respect women.

To my beloved Pastor Bishop Carlis L. Moody, Sr. who was the greatest gospel preacher in the world. He was the President of the International Missions Department of The Church of God in Christ for 40 years, but I simply called him "Dad". He strengthened me through my weakest hours; told me secrets that I refuse to write about, for they were only for my ears to cherish; and was a very affectionate and meek man who whooped you in a kind and caring way. People tried to take advantage of his kindness, but they soon realized that no man can be so weak, and yet establish churches in 100 countries. Whenever he saw me at the world conventions, no matter how important other dignitaries were who surrounded him, he always treated me as though I was the most important person in the room. His wife, Mother Mary Moody, is now the direct link to the heartbeat of this man and his legacy; she is indeed today's Mother of Zion.

Last but certainly not least, Lawrence Cleveland Jones, Jr. and Evelyn DeBerry Jones, or Dad and Mom (I saved these two for last because I wanted you to remember them the most). Chapter 7 in this book was easy to write because all I had to do was remember everything I saw in our house coming up between these two love birds. Married for over half a century, if you hung around them long enough, you would've thought they were still on their honeymoon. This may sound like a fairytale or a book of fiction, but Lawrence and Evelyn refused to fight in public, not even in front of us. My dad treated my Mom like royalty every single day and whenever we were outdoors, she was never allowed to touch a door handle or pick up anything heavy.

My dad was an Oldsmobile man and all 11 of us rode to church in that 4-door sedan Delta 88. Whenever we returned home from being at church for 12 hours, everybody exited the car BUT Mom, why? Because Dad would unlock the door to the house and tell us to do a walk through to make sure the entire house was safe. He then would tell one of us to "Go get your mother". We would open her door, escort her out and by the time she got to the stairs, he would say, "Ok boys, I got her from here". He would then wrap his arms around her until she was safely in the house. Funny thing about that story is that he still does this.

My mom had a fight with breast cancer some years ago and beat it but left the fight with debilitating injuries that weakened her to the point of needing wheel chair assistance. Did this stop my Father? Nope. Lawrence knew how to take those lemons and make lemonade! Whenever it was time for them to take a trip downtown or hide away in their timeshare, my dad literally picks my mom up with his bare hands to carry her. Never in my 50 plus years have I seen love like this.

Mom gave him 9 children, cooked, and cleaned. As a carpenter, he would sometimes come home after a 20-hour shift, and she would run to the window when she heard his muffler, meet him at the door with a kiss, usher him to the couch and sit on his lap and cuddle, no matter how smelly he was. Now that she's unable to run to him… he runs FOR her.

My parents' names aren't mentioned in chapter 7, but their story sure is, trust me, you'll spot it right away.

Table of Contents

Foreword

"The Four Women That Men Desire" by Sir Walter Jones, is an incredible integration of insight into the personalities of four women prototypes. Walter uses a holistic approach that addresses the physical, spiritual, and mental aspects that generate distinct personalities and behaviors of these women who he simply labels as Girl A, Girl B, Girl C, and Girl D.

Whether you have just recently entered into a new relationship, or are enjoying the longevity of a current relationship, or have just suffered a failed relationship, this book is replete with examples that explore relationship based concepts such as love, intimacy, forgiveness, integrity, compassion, deceit, commitment, infidelity, loyalty, etc. that will offer healing as well as understanding.

Walter has identified some of the key elements that are destroying the very fabric and foundation of our romantic relationships. He addresses the erosion of the sanctity of marriage, the dismantling of families after divorce, and the breakdown of communication among couples. The rudiments and values upon which relationships are built are disintegrating before our very eyes. However, within the pages of this book, Walter has prepared and delivered an affirming message that is highly effective in relaying and restoring those values.

One of the best features of *"The Four Women That Men Desire"* is the skillful manner in which Walter weaves his personal experiences into the book while providing actual case studies. This blend illuminates the topic, fully explores the subject matter, investigates the challenges, and offers an insightful "take-a-way" in each case. Readers will certainly identify with Walter as he revisits his own, personal pain while remaining transparent and candid.

Finally, Walter addresses what is possible when we are challenged to move away from our familiar thought patterns and confront and challenge irrational thoughts. In *"The Four Women That Men Desire"*, readers will learn how to identify the elements of growth in that process and transform the experience of change into one that opens new opportunities and improved relationships.

In a non-judgmental, conversational tone, Sir Walter Jones dispenses the knowledge and wisdom that will heal many people struggling in understanding the dynamics of their relationships. It is a book with a meaningful and timeless message.

Dr. Joyce A. Graham, M. Ed

Dr. Joyce A. Graham is a Licensed Professional Counselor. She completed her Master's Degree in Community Counseling at the University of Missouri-St. Louis. She currently has a private practice in Missouri where her counseling specialties include issues involving anxiety; depression; grief/loss; stress; and PTSD. For more on Dr. Graham, visit: www.betterhelp.com/joyce-graham/

Acknowledgments

Funny thing about acknowledgments...when you start calling out names, either you're going to forget to mention somebody or somebody is going to feel they should have been included. I thought of not having one of these pages to remedy this problem, however, the help I received on this book was too valuable for it to be omitted.

THE FAMILY

First of all, family means everything to me. I may not always call or hang out with them, but I surely will give up an arm, a leg or my life for them. My siblings have played a huge part in how I analyze women today and I would be remiss to not mention them. I first observed how my brothers treated the ladies and I followed suit. My father taught us to be gentlemen towards ladies and so the only times I've seen my brothers heated was when they were provoked – a couple of them had to make their beds on the rooftops next to Solomon though.
To Michael, Rodney, Larry, Dwayne, David, Justin, Janina and Precious, thank you for allowing me to observe your courting rituals.

I have adopted (stolen) several children and I made it my business to make sure they didn't repeat the mistakes I made in relationships. These children are always in my heart and in my mind and I'm forever grateful to their parents for allowing me some time with them. At the time of the release of this book, three of them are in college: Erick Reuben Tyson at Morehouse College (Psychology), Elyse Jeneene Tyson at Upper Iowa University (Mortuary Science) and Myleah Symone

Matheny at Judson University (Communication). My son Darious Thompson was the first one who taught me early in life how to love and protect a child and helped me understand why fathers are so important to boys/men.

Cozetta Jones gave me two amazing children who are the apple of my eye, the fruit of my labor and the reason behind my muse. Walter DeBerry Jones, Jr. is my hero, and everybody knows it. He is everything I was at his age; a true gentleman who loves his family and has always looked after his little sister. Rebecca Olivia Jones is my joy, my peace in the storm, she brightens up every room and SHE is the reason behind this book. Both are very independent, living on their own and showing the world who's boss. I'm the wealthiest man in town.

THE BACKERS

Although I used my own savings to write the book and hire key people in the business, I knew I would need to call out my Super Friends. Once I started to write, I stopped working and wasn't bringing in much income until I finished the book, so I needed help with strategic financing for marketing and promotions. Here's a list of my biggest donors who helped me stay nourished and kept the lights burning at 2am while I wrote; some gave multiple times and refused a repayment.

Amber Rogers
Lisa Johnson
Lana Wright
Dianne McDonald
Tony McClain
Barbara Taylor
Ora Cannady
Sharynna Allen-Ramsey

THE ENCOURAGERS

There's one person I know who was relentless every single day, from start to finish. Lady Reshell Dotson Matheny of Warriors Talk Radio, who I've known most of my adult life, emailed me faithfully at 12 noon to say, "It's time to write". I'm going to be honest and say that many times she got on my nerves and I just ignored her but look at me today! I will never forget her sacrifice and dedication.

Deatrice Carter, who sees Purity in all things (Titus 1:15), was my prayer warrior during this process. Victoria Jones-Dubose interceded on my behalf and would speak into my life through prayers in weekly videos. Demetria Brand Triplett and Kenyatta Masako Umphrey of "This Thing Called Life" Radio, kept me in check by always telling me the truth, no matter how much it hurt, yet remained among my biggest supporters. Demetra Williams Pitts was that person who made sure that not even my social media posts were sloppy. She ALWAYS made me look good in public. She was my one stop shop for everything promotional. She was quick, proficient, affordable, and a no-nonsense woman. I call her THE FIXER!!

THE BOYS CLUB

Robert "Buddy" Gill is my best friend. He knows more about me than my own brothers and has never left me. Even through the toughest times in my life, I could always count on him and his lovely wife Barbara for an embrace or some good, old-fashioned down home Soul Food. Alvin Carter was the co-host of my popular radio show, "The Sir Walter Jones Show"; he always knew when to make me laugh. I've told him both personally and publicly that he is one of the most Unsung Brilliant Minds of our time.

THE WORDSMITH

I have a lot of grammar kings and queens in my life, some I wish would just go away sometimes UNTIL I need to write a book...then they become the most important people in the whole wide world. One in particular is the International Award-Winning author and publisher, Toneal Monique Jackson. When the idea to write a book of this magnitude hit me like a ton of bricks, I searched my mind for someone experienced, somebody I'd be willing to submit myself to for guidance. No other name entered my mind but this great woman of God.

I'll never forget that day, driving in my car, too nervous to call her to even ask, for fear she'd turn me down. So instead of calling, I just shot her a Marco Polo video and waited with bated breath for the response. When she said yes, I knew at that moment that this was going to be a bumpy ride for me. Why? Because Toneal is known as THE BOSS! During this process, I remember walking in her office (APS Bookstore's Chicago location) with my manuscripts, shaking in my boots, knowing she was about to send me back home crying, insisting I redo EVERYTHING. Sometimes, she would respond with a "Naw, that ain't gonna work in the literary world"; but then, my good days would come with her saying, "OMG, you're a freaking GENIUS".

I never knew how valuable structural editors were until I walked into this woman's office. Toneal can take a lonely box of Jiffy Mix and transform it into steak and potatoes. I always felt like I was in English class 101 around her, but because I enjoy learning, I soaked it all up and can now present to you this book – some of my best work, all because I had the greatest teacher and editor in the world.

Author's Note

Many people asked why I chose to write a book of this nature – a controversial text that is sure to upset both men and women alike. Men, because it can be perceived that I am exposing the brotherhood; women, because the notion is that I am being unnecessarily judgmental. If you know me, you know that I didn't take the time to explain myself or my rationale because my work speaks for itself. But if you don't know me...

My name is Sir Walter Jones, and I'd like to think of this book as my story, my brothers' story, my sons' story, oh, and my father's story. To be honest with you, it's the story of every man who has ever shown interest in a woman.

Ironically enough, much of my motivation behind writing this book stems from the fact that I not only am a father to a son, but also a daughter. One day, I was having a conversation with Rebecca Olivia (my daughter), asking her about boys. During this conversation, I noticed her mannerisms, her innocence and purity, which kind of reminded me of my first love.

In that moment, I wondered, "How do boys see my daughter? Do they see her the way I see women?" It killed me that I didn't know, but I figured writing a book that explains how men perceive women would help address this for other parents as well.

Another reason for this book is to set the record straight regarding relationship statuses. Most people in my circle believe that there are seven women to one man (an Isaiah 4:1 reference), and thus, women have no choice but to settle when it comes to men and relationships. However, when you look at the actual statistics of women to men ratio that are born, it's almost half and half. So, it's not about physical body count; it is more about availability.

According to relationship expert Gary Chapman, there are Five Love Languages; Mitch Albom discusses The Five People You Meet in Heaven. Well, Sir Walter has concluded (after years of living with my mom and sisters, having several girlfriends and two failed marriages) that there are only FOUR women that men desire. My hope is that this book will allow you to see through my mind's eye, the experiences of myself and other men to better understand why we choose the women we do. The choices are not always clear-cut; neither do they always result in a happy ending. Case and point, Valentine's Day 2009...

I was living in a town outside of Fort Lauderdale, Florida, with an old college friend, he was my best friend. I was staying with him because at the time I was stagnant; I was uncertain of what I was going to do with my life. For the first time in 10 years, there was no woman in my life.

My friend asked if I had plans for Valentine's Day because he and his fiancée wanted to spend time alone in the house. I made up some story saying that I had plans with a woman from the church, which was a total lie. I didn't have plans, neither did I have a car, so I ended up walking the streets all night.

I walked a couple of miles, found a park, sat on a swing, and began talking to myself, then to God. I wondered how could a guy like me, who had so much going for himself be 1,400 miles from home and alone on Valentine's Day? I talked, cried, walked in circles, and then it dawned on me. I'd written this song in 1995 that perfectly described my current situation – as if it was prophetic. It was called You Will Never Be Alone. I believe God brought those lyrics back to me:

One night I was walking in the park
Seeing couples holding hands, embracing in the dark
As they kissed, I wondered, Why not me? Why can't it be?
Oh, Lord, could you please comfort me?

I thought, "Nobody who wants to be loved should experience what I'm experiencing now". I felt the need, even then to do something to create a solution. Someone had to address this problem – why do we love, lose love, or fall out of love? Once you finish reading this book, you should have a better handle on the answers.

Introduction

I have always been a man who observed numbers – I even dabbled in numerology. While reading the Bible, I noticed a pattern with God and numbers. I have always liked the number seven and what it represents (completion) and realized that I'd subconsciously been implementing it in my daily life – especially in music. So, I decided to continue with this model for my books. There are seven volumes; seven chapters in each volume; and seven subchapters in each chapter.

This volume is purposed to not only be used as a self-reflective tool for the individual reader, but also to promote dialogue between couples, and even discussion groups. Regardless of gender, I have noticed as it pertains to relationships, the same question is posed repeatedly: "Why do I keep attracting the same type of person?" In reading and dissecting this book, my hope is you will ascertain a greater understanding. However, I realize that many will misinterpret the information.

Have you ever had a rash form on your body or maybe even an uncontrollable cough and instead of calling a doctor you went straight to Google? You typed what seemed to be your symptoms and the search brought you to a disease where the symptoms were like yours, so you concluded you had this deadly disease and totally freaked out? I can assure you that many will treat this book the same way; I caution you though to read the entire text before making any self-diagnosis!

While you're reading, I want you to keep in mind that this book is not about what's right or wrong; it just explains what is. I have found that most times, people already know the difference between right and wrong.

As an example, if I told you that adultery was wrong, you'd probably turn a deaf ear, wouldn't you? Why? Because you already know that it's wrong, so having someone seemingly condemn you wouldn't help the situation. However, if I showed you how continuing may lead you to a destructive path of no return, that may prove more effective. So, while this is not written to condemn, if you possess a desire to make changes in your life, the final chapter will contain some suggestions. My goal, as with any counselor, is not to solve your problem, but to empower you to solve your own problem!

Another word of caution. Women, it may appear to you in certain instances that some of the girls in the book are portrayed as meat – this is no coincidence. Whereas, it is not my intent to be offensive, there are times when using animal references adequately explain the behavior of men, and some women too. To be honest with you, they need to consider filming an Animal Planet, PBS Nature or National Geographic episode in our churches, airports, grocery stores and places of employment because if you ever just sit in a chair with a bowl of popcorn and watch humans interact with each other, you just might be surprised to see the similarities.

Case and point, I was watching National Geographic, and they showed a hungry leopard approaching a dead carcass; he sniffed it but wouldn't touch it. The narrator said because the leopard didn't kill it himself, he wouldn't eat it for fear that it may be diseased. The narrator also said that this predator will, after rejecting a dead carcass, stalk its prey for miles. When it finally catches it, it will take it up a tree and eat it there. Why? It wants to eat it undisturbed, so it takes it off the food market. I'm often amazed at how even though man has dominion over the Animal Kingdom, wildlife often shows greater restraint.

Finally, I'd like to leave you with some cliff notes, or what I like to call, *Sir Walter's Seven Takeaways*:

1) **General House Rule – Read the text with an open mind understanding that some of these traits are interchangeable depending on the woman.** When you get stuck on a girl that you have already concluded that may or may not be you, do me a favor. Go back to the cover and read (and reread) the title. Every time I am invited to a woman's forum where men are the panelists, a woman always asks the man to give his honest opinion, and without fail, the woman disagrees with his answer. I think to myself, "Why call all these men here if you're not going to believe this is their truth. Whether it's right or wrong, this is how they feel". This book is called The Four Women that Men Desire for a reason; it's from the perception of a man – not a woman! So, if you are as pretty and sexy as Girl D, and then read that she has a mental dysfunction ("Spoiler Alert"), don't conclude that men have misread you. There's a possibility that you are not that girl.

2) **When Sex is Your Superpower – This woman may possess different talents and skills, however, she is mostly valued because of her sexual abilities and limitless desire to please her man.** Have you ever heard the old saying, "A man wants a lady in the street but a freak in the sheets"? This is the first type of woman you are going to encounter in Volume 1 of The Men's

Chronicles. She inflicts low to no standards, which makes her easy to lead on. Although there is little likelihood that she will become his wife, she enjoys the thought of the possibility.

3) **When Brains and Beauty are Your Birthright – This woman is desired because her presence brings bragging rights.** Every man wants someone who not only makes him look good, but also makes him the envy of his friends. She is a triple threat – brains, beauty, and the ability to boost his ego. Although she may not become his wife, they both enjoy fantasizing about the future.

4) **The Interlude – An intervening period.** I felt the need to include the interlude to provide a transitional explanation, just as you would see in a movie or play. Embrace it as it gives you the opportunity to meditate on the message.

5) **When Cooking is Your Calling – Every man wants this woman.** Other than his mother, in his eyes, there is no one better. Who else can and will selflessly cook, clean, and take care of him, his house and his children? He values her and everything she brings to the table. She is his safe haven.

6) **When You're Dangerously Desperate – Too much of anything can be a bad thing – or in this case, a dangerous thing.** Whereas a man doesn't mind having a woman who wants to be his everything, with this woman, he must be

careful. Everything just may cost him his life...literally!

7) **The Renewed Mind – Always be willing to challenge yourself to learn from life and think about things from multiple perspectives.** While every woman has a strength, it is important to note that the purpose of this book is not to assess the woman as she sees herself; rather to provide perspective from a man's per view. It's necessary to understand that men are fleshly creatures, meaning that we see first with our eyes and then with our hearts. The order in which the women are presented is representative of how they are perceived by men. Initially, we ingest a woman's body, then her beauty, then ultimately determine if we desire a deeper relationship. The more you live, the more you learn. From your experiences, as well as those from family, friends, neighbors, co-workers, etc. While learning from others is great, always be willing to allow the Bible to teach you some of your essential lessons.

Chapter One:
Birth Order

"How parents interact with each child as it enters the family circle determines in great part that child's final destiny." – Dr. Kevin Leman

It's amazing how one sentence can perfectly explain everything that has happened to you. Did it ever occur to you that the things you experience in life can all be traced back to your birth order? Not just the type of job you go after, but even the kinds of relationships you pursue can all be determined simply by your place in your family circle.

I was skeptical too at first, but attending a seminar hosted by the Father of Birth Order, world-renowned Christian author, Dr. Kevin Leman made me a believer. At this event, Dr. Leman gave the attendees a quiz comprised of a list of personality traits. We were charged to label them from A-D, which would help the good doctor determine whether we happened to be the firstborn; last born; middle child or only child. He did let us know that some qualities could overlap, but overall, just by knowing the types of jobs we had or personality traits we possessed, he could predict our birth order.

Someone's quiz revealed they were the CEO of a company, and Dr. Leman correctly predicted that he was a firstborn. He informed us that "statistics show that firstborns often fill positions of high authority or achievement". I couldn't believe it – he was spot on with just about everybody, men and women alike...everyone except me that is!

He explained that predicting middle children is always his most difficult task because they are all so different. Depending on the number of years that separate them from their siblings, they can mimic the behavior of a firstborn, last born or only child. He said that the middle child can be "a maverick with many friends. Usually the one to leave home first. The one who finds real companionship outside the family circle because he often feels sort of left out of things at home". And although he may not have guessed my birth order correctly, his explanation fit me to a tee.

You see, I am a middle child. There is one and a half years between me and my older brother. So, for a while, I was treated like the baby. I didn't have to do all the things that were expected of Michael, Rodney, and Larry (my older brothers). But once my brother Dwayne was born, I was expected to help my mom take care of him. In fact, it seemed like almost every year an additional baby came along that I had to make bottles for or help change. If it wasn't Dwayne, it was David or Justin or Janina or Precious that needed me. I soon missed my years of being spoiled. I had my parents to myself four years before Dwayne was born. So, it hit home when Dr. Leman spoke of how the middle child could be mistaken for the others because I'd experienced being treated like both the youngest and the oldest.

My encounter with Dr. Leman had such a profound impact. The more I listened to him discuss this birth order phenomenon, the more I reflected on other aspects – namely the relationships I'd engaged in throughout my life. I began to think about the birth orders of these women to help identify their traits. And it seemed that with this new information, I was now equipped to understand why my relationships failed.

I began to examine the different women I'd been involved with. I recalled the number of women who were middle children, like me. I remember Dr. Leman describing this child as "being known for going in exactly the opposite direction from the firstborn in the family". He characterized middle children as being mediators. "A real paradox, independent, but with extreme loyalty to his peer group".

Then I thought about all the firstborns I dated as well as those who were born last or were the only child. After realizing their birth order and associated traits, not only did I know why I was attracted to them, but I could also categorize them into types – four types to be exact. The next chapters you read will describe these women and explain the characteristics they possess that deem them desirable.

Chapter Two:
Girl A (The Side Chick)

Walk in any public place where it's mostly women and you will easily spot a *Girl A*. She's there, blending in with the crowd...UNTIL a man enters. She may not have come there looking for him, but now that he's there, he becomes the center of her attraction. The #MeToo Movement has caused many to focus exclusively on the men as predators, all while Girl A slips through the cracks.

For many years I was called a "Church Pimp". I heard it so much until I believed it. However, when I look back on several of the women I dated (all the way back to high school), I discovered this pattern.

There were times when I would be at church sitting on the piano, minding my own business, and would often be approached by them. I was either invited over for dinner; brought a plate of food; or had a hotel key shoved in my pocket. Being young and feeling lonely, I usually took the bait and found myself repenting later. Sure, there were those I approached myself, but it was more the exception to the rule. This behavior led me to wonder, "How can I be the pimp when they were coming after me? Do prostitutes find their pimps?"

After my divorce, I just knew I was done with women. I remember telling God that I was going to dedicate myself to the music ministry, teaching, and fatherhood. I then remember being invited to a singles' gathering. It was held in a woman's home among friends. We had such a great time filled with food, laughter and love. For the first time in years I felt like I belonged.

Hours later, I found myself waking up on the couch only to discover that everyone else had left – everyone except the homeowner. As I got up to leave, she asked if I would stay a little longer. I politely refused, explaining that I had a long drive ahead. As I reached for the door, she reached for my zipper and belt buckle; I had to wrestle her hands away. What happened next not only altered my future for years to come, it also gave me a clearer look into how women think (I'll explain more on that in Volume 6).

But for now, let's take a closer look at Girl A: The Side Chick...

The Profile – Also known as "The Side Chick", a man desires this woman because the sexual encounters with her are extremely gratifying. It is mutually understood that she only serves one purpose in his life. They have a "no strings attached" relationship.

1. Sexually Satisfying – The Freak

    a) Readily available when called (booty call):

    - They have sex any time, any place.

    - Privacy is not important.

    - She will do whatever it takes (to a point) to satisfy his sexual appetite.

    - They have a predictable sexual routine (specific day and time). She believes that she's wife material even to the point of referring to herself as 'wifey'.

    - Psychology of Man: He's a creature of habit. The nature of him is to get his release. He doesn't care if it's boring to her. He manipulates her to believe that it's what she wants.

    b) Fulfills his sexual desires (she is his sexual fantasy):

    - She will comply to his desired positions (oral and anal sex are allowed)

    - Ménage trois is acceptable. Even if her feelings get in the way, he will continue having sex with the other partner, which is usually another Girl A.

    - She allows herself to be dominated, but doesn't stand for BDSM

c)   **He comes to her house for sex:**

- He may have a key to her home, but he will never give her a key to his place for fear that she may pop up at any time. I had a woman come over to my house; at the time I lived in a two-level townhouse. I excused myself from the living room to go to the restroom only to return and find her missing. I went upstairs and found her in my bedroom looking through my closet. I showed her the door and never allowed her back. From that point, all our sexual escapades convened at her house.

- He doesn't bring her to his home ever because he has multiple women and doesn't want any surprise visits.

- He wants to maintain his image within the neighborhood. He doesn't want them to see women going in and out of his home.

- He might be married so he either goes to her house or a "four-hour block" neighborhood hotel; never a five-star.

- Since he only wants her for sex, once it's over, he wants to be able to leave immediately after.

- She has more food in her house.

- He leaves clothes there for convenience – not because they are in a committed relationship. He needs somewhere to change so as not to reveal his prior activities.

- She will NEVER have clothes at his house.

d) **Rumored from his friends that she's good in bed:**

- This man chases her because she sounds like someone who would fit his fantasy based on what a family member (usually a male sibling) or his friends have said. In extreme cases, two brothers can knowingly share the same girl.

- *The Grass is Always Greener Effect* – He may already have a girlfriend but wants to experience her for himself and not just rely on friends' accounts. He fails to realize that hearts are attached. There may be issues that he doesn't want to be associated with and must decide if sleeping with her is worth the trouble.

- Psychology of Envy: Envy is its own psychology and is one of the seven deadly sins in Christianity. Anyone who has ever read *Dante's Divine Comedy* knows a little about the subject of Invidia (Latin for a sense of envy; a "looking upon" associated with the evil eye). I remember when I bought my beautiful 2014 Ford Fusion. I drove it off the lot and the same make and model drove past me traveling much faster. The only difference between the cars was the color – it was white and mine was black. So why did I want to drive it so badly? I believe that envy is placed in us at birth. I learned the best way to remove a toy from a child's hand is to replace it with another.

e)   **Doesn't have to be wined and dined:**

- She isn't used to being taken to nice places, social events, etc.; clubs and house parties are her usual scene. Because she's not used to it, she doesn't look for it. He knows this and therefore creates a "role play" atmosphere by making her home "the place to be".

- She likes cheap alcohol.

f)   **Has had several boyfriends/partners:**

- *The Misery Loves Company Effect* – Girl A is not satisfied with herself. She chooses/attracts the same kind of man. Misery indeed loves company, but a certain "type" of company. Men who are predators will prey on the same type of woman, just as a woman who is preyed on, falls for the same type of guy.

- She has possibly been molested or had other traumatic sexual experiences in her childhood. In my many counseling sessions, I have discovered that the subject of inappropriate touching always pops up with my clients. It's either a father touching his children; a mother touching her son; a mother's lover touching her children; aunts, uncles, cousins or a family friend who is the molester or rapist. Too many families today have major sexual coverups that have been kept secret for generations.

- She lacks parental love, and thus is "looking for love in all the wrong places".

- The men have other relationships and only see her as a "Girl A". In his other relationships, the women supply his missing pieces; he needs Girl A for his physical release.

- She's frequented clinics for STDs, abortions and other health issues. Although later in life she got on some type of birth control, she never required her sexual partners to use protection.

g)   **Probably a single mother:**

- Even if she has other men in and out, she's not married.

- She probably has more than one child, all in public schools.

- The fathers are not in the lives of the children.

- *The ACE Effect* – She was probably part of a broken home growing up. The Adverse Childhood Experiences (ACE) study, which was conducted by the American Health Maintenance Organization, The Kaiser Permanente and the Centers for Disease Control and Prevention, found that childhood experiences, both positive and negative, have a tremendous impact on future violence victimization and perpetration, and lifelong health and opportunity.

2. **She Knows Her Role – The Side Chick**

   a) **She won't call, text, or do anything to mess up the "integrity" of his relationship:**

   - At some point, she lives in a world of make believe and refers to him as her man or mate knowing that there is no future.

   b) **He's married or has a significant other:**

   - He never had to remove his wedding ring upon meeting her.

   - She knows his wife/partner and remains cordial with her at public events.

c) She respects who he is and is flattered at the opportunity to be with someone "like him":

- He literally has a spell on her and she knows it. Like a drug, she enjoys it.

d) She understands that she won't spend actual holiday time with him:

- The day before or the day after holidays and his birthday is the established time they will spend together. The actual day will never belong to her.

- If she is married, the same rules apply.

e) She will babysit the children he has from another relationship:

- Part of her altered reality is to believe and treat his children as theirs.

- The children, if old enough to talk, refer to her as "aunt".

f) She's aware but doesn't care because she's getting something out of the relationship:

- The family attachment makes her feel that he's safe and secure.

g) The only one she can talk to is her best friend because she understands the "relationship" and helps to protect it:

- Her friend is the spitting image of her.

3. She's A Giver – The Sugar Momma

a) She gives him herself – mind, body and soul. She withholds nothing; freely discusses future, family, dreams, etc.:

- She worships the ground he walks on.

- She would move closer to him and remain the side chick.

b) She is willing to sacrifice herself and all she has for him:

- Even to the point of doing something illegal or life-threatening

- She will neglect her children for him

c) She exhibits some qualities of Girl C:

- If she's married, she's her husband's Girl C

- Some days, he actually feels a temporary connection with her. A good feeling comes over him because some things she says and does trigger his heart.

d) She gives her time; she will rearrange her schedule to be with him:

- She will call in sick or may call off work just to be with him

- He is the center of her attraction and he comes before anyone else

e) **She always has food:**

- She came from a broken home, so food was scarce and now she overcompensates.

- She cooks fast foods, microwaveable dishes, and other items deemed unhealthy.

f) **She gives her heart. She loves him but doesn't love herself:**

- She sometimes cries during sex or an intimate moment.

- She will do whatever he says (cut/grow her hair; gain/lost weight, etc.) to please him.

g) **She is his "petty cash" chick. He knows she doesn't have a lot of money to give:**

- When he needs gas money, bus fare, pocket change, or even something for his home/family, he will ask her.

4. **No Emotional Involvement**

a) **He doesn't care about her well-being:**

- There are more fish in the sea. She holds no true value with him.

- If she's sick, he won't tend to her because he can't be seen taking her to the doctor/hospital.

b) **He doesn't call to see about her unless it's to get something from her:**

- She's the cleanup woman; he needs a place to stay (temporarily).

c) **He doesn't care about her children:**

- When he comes over, he prefers them to be gone or preoccupied in their room.

- He won't do anything fun with them unless it's beneficial for him.

d) **He doesn't volunteer to be a physical presence in her life:**

- He doesn't want to become emotionally attached.

- He realizes her problems will become his so he's reluctant to help.

e) **He refuses to meet any of her family members:**

- He fears that one of them may know someone he knows.

- It may emphasize that things are getting serious.

- Her family will now be watching him.

- They will invite him to family gatherings.

f) **He can't pray with or for her:**

- He can't pray with her because he's sinning.

- Praying with her is an emotional attachment; he doesn't have that or want that with her.

- It brings about conviction and he doesn't want to convict her heart because he doesn't want her to do right.

g) **He doesn't like pillow talk:**

- He doesn't discuss his goals and dreams with her because she has no value to him.

- After he climaxes, he only wants to sleep

- She wants to talk, so he will just so as not to bite the hand that feeds him. He knows that if he doesn't talk to her, she won't have sex with him.

5. Looks are not Important – The Vagina has No Face

a) Conforms to his lustful desires:

- He makes her feel like she's sexy, but uses ecstasy and erotica, not romance. He doesn't say "let's make love"; he is blunt and profane with her. She doesn't know the difference between the two.

b) He only sees her as a tool to satisfy his flesh:

- She has slightly more value to him than a blow-up doll.

- *The Bathroom Effect* – See the urinal. Use the urinal. You don't have the desire to use the restroom until you see the urinal. Some men don't want to have sex until they see Girl A because she reminds him of pornographic images and stirs the lust in him. Also, he figuratively dumps all over her.

- She scratches all his itches. She satisfies all his fetishes.
  - ➢ Toe sucking
  - ➢ Anal licking
  - ➢ Oral sex

c) She dresses like a whore, which reveals her vulnerability:

- She wears colored wigs; contacts; makeup, etc.

- She thinks she's beautiful. She has conformed to how she believes a beautiful woman looks.

d) **He will not take pictures with her:**

- He has an image to uphold

- He's afraid of leaks; he doesn't want her sharing pics

- He doesn't want to encourage this behavior because it affirms that they are a couple; in his mind they are not.

e) **The only pictures he has of her are of them having sex:**

- When he has an itch that needs to be scratched, those pictures help him to masturbate.

- He has a private video stash of them having sex on his phone or computer.

- He shows the pictures to a trusted friend for bragging rights or another Girl A to serve as motivation for their sexual escapades.

f) **He doesn't take her out in public:**

- He's afraid that they might see someone that one of them know; their relationship must remain a secret.

- If he does, it's a neighborhood locale.

- If he eats at his favorite restaurant, it can only be takeout because he doesn't want to be recognized.

- He considers her "low-class" so he's only going to spend a small amount of money on her.

- If they do go out, it's far away (another city or town)

g) **She could be toothless, and it wouldn't matter:**

- She's not a healthy eater, nor does she care to know what ruins her teeth.

- When he first met her and saw her smile, he is immediately able to identify her as a Girl A. Research has proven that men really value the state of a woman's teeth, but she is the exception to the rule.

- He only kisses her during sex to pacify her and/or connect "marginal points" of kissing and penetrating

- He sees her and determines she is probably good at oral sex.

6. She's Uneducated – Ghetto Mentality

a) Barely finished high school; possible dropout:

- She was probably raised in a single-parent home and was a latch key kid.

- She spent her school years making friends and trying to impress others.

- If she dropped out, she stayed home and had babies with different guys.

- She reads and writes at an elementary level and probably got promoted because of social passing (No Child Left Behind).

b) Was a teen mom:

- She loves her firstborn but neglect subsequent children.

- Heavily relies on governmental assistance to take care of her children (public aid; WIC; etc.).

c) Doesn't speak proper English:

- She speaks in present-day colloquialisms and ebonics.

- She posts on social media the same way she talks.

d) Unable to have an intelligent conversation:

- She's angry/jealous of her peers who have excelled.

- She's unable to quote from anyone other than an entertainer.

- She doesn't know anything about current events or breaking news unless it's a scandal, on reality television, or social media.

e) **He doesn't seek advice from her:**

- The Dumb Blonde Effect – He sees her as having no intellectual value

- There is no pillow talk, and if it is she's gossiping. He only listens; he doesn't actively engage or reciprocate dialogue.

f) **Her friends are just like her (birds of a feather):**

- These were her school friends. Some finished, some didn't.

- She's always on the phone or social media with them planning unproductive activities.

- They talk her into doing things that keep her in a state of social despair.

  - How she dresses
  - Leaving her children with her parents so she can go out

g)   **She doesn't have a conventional job:**

- She receives governmental assistance

- The highlight of her month is the 1st when she receives her check. She's "hood rich". To her, this is good money, but she consumes it quickly.

- She doesn't have a bank account.

  ➢ She only uses cash or prepaid debit cards

  ➢ Her financial interactions are limited (she can't cash checks without going to a check cashing business.

- She has a low credit score/subprime credit lending.

  ➢ She uses Rent-to-Own and Title Loan businesses

  ➢ If she has a car, it's with the type of companies that will repossess it or shut it off from the company's headquarters.

- She doesn't know about investments, stocks, etc.

7. **She Will NEVER Meet Anyone He's Close to…ESPECIALLY His Mother – The Embarrassment**

a)   He won't introduce the two even if they are
     in the same room

b)   She is the antithesis of his mother:

     • She's low-class

     • She's not nurturing

     • She wouldn't be celebrated the way his
       mother is celebrated among family.

c)   The mother will only see a "street girl" when
     looking at her:

     • He feels she only dresses one way –
       provocative.

     • That street girl persona attracted him,
       but will repel his mother.

d)   She is incapable of holding a conversation
     with his mother:

     • Regardless of her race/culture, she is
       the lowest class and speaks accordingly.

e)   He knows that his family will automatically
     embrace her as a sister; he knows that she
     doesn't meet the family standard:

     • They will receive her because they love
       him; he knows they will secretly judge
       him in a negative manner.

f) Because of her perceived behavior, it's possible that she has had (or would have) sexual relations with his friends:

- She is his possession and he knows that men will be men – even though it's his friends. Why? Because he knows himself.

g) He doesn't like to cross worlds:

- His co-workers are not close enough to implement discretion, and he doesn't want to chance this relationship going public.

- He feels his co-workers are incapable of keeping up with his affairs and may wreak havoc on his social life confusing names and faces.

Chapter Three:
Girl B (The Mistress)

Hey brothers, have you ever walked in a public place and saw a woman that was so beautiful, that you immediately became intimidated? "Surely a woman that FINE wouldn't give me the time of day" you thought. She must be happily married. You begin to try and psychoanalyze the situation by inserting the "what ifs", concluding to yourself that it wouldn't work because she's probably crazy.

This always makes you feel better about walking away and possibly averting a time bomb explosion. I set a rat trap one night, sat back and waited awhile for it to grab the cheese. It did, and the trap snapped on its head. I then saw that bloody faced rat pick the trap up, sling it and scurry off. I reset the trap and hours later that same rat came back to try it again. Why? Because that cheese was just too irresistible. Girl B drives men WILD and whenever she's in the room, it's like nobody else matters. As much as he may try and play it off and look away, she's the moon and he's the high tide.

I've dated Girl Bs in the past and discovered so many similarities among them; it's almost like they were raised up in the same home. Notice how I'm calling her the "Backup Plan". Being the Mistress and not the Side Chick, she actually has a chance to win over his hear.t Out of the other women featured in this volume, Girl B is the one for whom he would leave his wife. Look at pop culture, politics, education and even the clergy; men in these arenas have literally divorced their wives and married this woman. Notice when you hear of a scandal among powerful men, how it's the Girl B type that gets the most publicity and not a Girl A. The wife knows that Girl A was just a flesh thing, but Girl B was a HEART thing, which is why she will ask him "Do You Love Her"?

I have literally taken a 24-hour Greyhound Bus ride one way to be with a Girl B because what was drawing me was not the sex as much as it was the fantasy. Men lie about their assets when they're with her; they drop famous names; they go into debt to try to impress her long enough to work out his distorted world and Ponzi Scheme.

The Philosopher Thomas Carlyle once wrote, "For if there be a Faith, from of old, it is this, as we often repeat, that no lie can live forever" (The French Revolution. A History 1837, Part 1, Book VI, chapter 3).

So, without further ado, meet Girl B...

The Profile – Known as "The Mistress" this is the woman that a man will leave his wife for. He is totally engrossed in her beauty, and her superficiality appeals to him. He thinks of her as his *Backup Plan*.

1. He MIGHT Leave His Wife for Her

    a)   They do partner activities:

- house shopping
- joint accounts

    b)   They go on exotic trips together:

- His accompaniment on the trips further solidifies in her mind that one day he will leave his wife for her.

- Travelling fulfills her fantasies

    c)   He keeps clothes at her house:

- It's convenient for him

- It sends a message of security to her

- Depending on how toxic things are at home, he has an exit plan to leave the wife to be with her.

- He slowly removes inconspicuous items from the house; he knows one day soon the inevitable will occur.

    d)   He complains about his wife to her:

- *The Lady in Waiting Effect* – She must always stay one step ahead. He verbally compares her to his wife to keep her hopes up.

e)   **They discuss moving in together:**

- He periodically talks about how he will take a room (of her home or a new place) to remodel it as a man cave or office.

f)   **They always talk about getting married:**

- He uses vernacular with more certainty to help reassure her ("when" instead of "if").

g)   **They talk about having a family:**

- If she already has children, he is present in their lives and they have already fallen for him. An emotional attachment is formed.

- Although he may not want any children, he will allow her to bring up the subject.

2.   **She's Educated**

a)   **She's a CEO (has a high-paying job):**

- ***The Hitchhiker Effect*** – I always enjoyed watching movies on the Turner Classic Movie channel. I noticed whenever they showed a hitchhiker, she was always wearing a skirt or showing her legs to get the cars to stop. This girl is a charmer. Some of her opportunities arise because of her looks.

b) **She has influence:**

- *The Olivia Pope Effect* – On the ABC political drama series, Scandal, Olivia Pope (played by Kerry Washington) is a crisis manager based in Washington, DC., who has her own firm. She is a fixer and she often successfully makes political problems go away. How is she able to do this? Through the influence she possesses.

c) **She's ambitious:**

- *The Being Mary Jane Effect* – Mary Jane Paul, "Pauletta", (played by Gabrielle Union) is a successful TV news anchor for Satellite News Channel. Her family is not very supportive of her life choices, yet she remains persistent and resilient, but like Olivia Pope, can't get her love life in order.

  ➢ She's married to her job
  ➢ She doesn't have many friends

d) **Possibly valedictorian or salutatorian:**

- She was the most popular and/or most hated girl in school.

- Her parents stressed perfect grades and rewarded her for it.

e) **Voted "Most Likely to Succeed":**

- She always presided over a club or organization at school.

f) **She's a college graduate:**

- She may have made a career of going to school.

- She doesn't know how to cultivate a relationship.

- She has dry humor and doesn't know how to laugh at "regular" or everyday situations.

- She only speaks about scholarly topics.

g) **She's always one step ahead of him:**

- She learned about business and economics by studying "how-to" material and dating businessmen.

3. **She is High Maintenance**

a) *The Golden Rectangle Effect – She's eye candy.* In Geometry class, I learned about the Golden Rectangle Formula. It was one of the most boring classes ever, but once I started to study Psychology and Sociology, I began to see a pattern in the behavior of humankind. Beauty cannot be judged objectively, hence the saying, "Beauty is in the eye of the beholder". But is this true? Today, we see a trend that seems to rebel against this theory by paying attention to how companies sell to consumers through media. So many things fit in that "Golden Rectangle" – books, iPads, credit cards, even women. There is a universal envy that we all have by what we see. It's not subjective anymore; we want to possess what everyone loves to look at.

- ➤ She wears modest makeup. She doesn't look like a clown or dead person.

- ➤ She has a beautifully, dazzling smile.

- ➤ She meets his height requirements.

- ➤ *Social Media Profile Pics/Catfishing* – This happened to me. I talked on the phone for weeks with someone and fell in love with her voice; it was alluring. We discussed physical appearance and she admitted she was a little overweight. However, when I saw her in person, I discovered that she was morbidly obese. I had to find a polite way to end our interactions.

b)   **She has a beautiful complexion:**

- *The "Eye of the Beholder" Effect* – In my travels and discussion with men of different races, I noticed that their taste in complexion and shade can vary, but slightly. Most Americans prefer dating and marrying within their race, but the gap is closing in, especially post Obama years. The beauty industry and magazines dictate to us what is considered attractive, yet in the real world, men still go with their own gauge.

c)   **He is fixated on her body parts:**

- Although stereotype studies say black men may be more attracted to her derriere, white men to her breasts, Latino men to her legs, and Asian men to her height, I believe that what attracts a man to a woman is a case by case basis. When he sees her for the first time, his eyes will focus on "his" preferred spot.

- Typically, when watching tv shows, appealing refers to tall, skinny, long legs, naturally (looking) long hair.

- He considers noticeable blemishes (freckles, moles, birthmarks, etc.) beauty marks.

d)   **She walks like a lady:**

- *The Clydesdale Effect* – These women are admired by men because of their long legs and the way they strut.

- *The Peacock Effect* – She is poised; walks with dignity; has a subtle switch. In the Bible, Solomon compares the Shulamite woman to Pharaoh's Chariots, "You are as exciting, my darling, as a mare among Pharaoh's stallions" (Song of Songs 1:9).

e)   **She gives him bragging rights:**

- In his mind, she's the most beautiful woman in the room.

- Having her boosts his ego because he feels he has a competitive edge. Even if he's insecure, he wants other men to want what he has.

- He views her as his possession. If no one wants her, he doesn't feel empowered.

- *You Remind Me of My Jeep Effect* – In 1995, R&B singer R. Kelly released a self-titled album with the hit song, *You Remind Me of My Jeep.* The lyrics left nothing to the imagination; scintillating and filled with double entendres, the raunchy tune perfectly captured how men compare their women to objects or possessions they cherish most.

f) **She has pretty hands:**

- She doesn't do manual labor

- She keeps nail files, clippers, polish, etc. on hand.

- She won't scratch his back for fear of breaking a nail.

g) **She has many clothes:**

- She shops at boutiques. Her clothes are original.

- She is a fashionista

- She's a trendsetter
    - Paris Hilton
    - Kim Kardashian
    - Nikki Minaj
    - Beyonce
    - Jennifer Lopez

4. She's A Gold Digger

a) **She's used to men wining and dining her:**

- She knows men may be intimidated to date her.

- When men approach her, they automatically presume that she's high-end, classy or high-maintenance. They push through their fear for chance she will say yes to a date. They know they must BRING IT.

- Men know not to insult her with street talk or petty pickup lines, so they tread carefully.

- He brags and/or lies about his accomplishments just to impress her.

b) **She likes name brands (upscale):**

- She was raised to appreciate the finer things in life.

- If she didn't have them growing up, she promised herself that she would have them once she got older.

- She may be living above her means, but she knows she must uphold her image.

- Because she was given these things before, she now feels she can't live without them.

c) **She likes to travel:**

- She sees travelling as being romantic and exotic.

- She feels "it's what wealthy people do."

- She thinks if you can travel, you have arrived.

- Once she travelled the first time, she exaggerates her experiences to continue to build this image that men have bought into.

d) **She has a sugar daddy:**

- She's between 25-35 years old

- She will do whatever it takes to make cash flow.

e) **She's selfish:**

- She must be included on his shopping sprees. He can't bring home any personal items unless he has something for her.

- She's always been a taker – not a giver, so she really doesn't know how to celebrate others.

- *The Noel Jones Effect* – He had a Girl B, who wanted more from the relationship. He went to counseling to better himself and she was frustrated because it had nothing to do with her. It was about HIS improvement not THEIR improvement.

f) **She's in love with the ring:**

- She doesn't care about his heart

- She obsessed with a wedding – not marriage.

- She may have been married before

- She's a bridezilla

g) **She never carries cash – credit cards only:**

- She understands the mindset of the rich, so she tries to emulate them even if she's not rich.

- Paris Hilton once ran out of gas. She received help from a stranger and gave him a $20 bill. When he brought back change, she threw it in her back seat, totally repulsed by having to touch it.

5.   **She's Not Domestic**

a)   **She was spoiled all her life:**

- She had an overly protective parent who either hired people to do chores or the parent did the chores.

b)   **She was in beauty contests (pageant queen):**

- She was raised to believe that she is a princess/queen, and all are to admire her. Pageant participation was a perfect way to attain this goal.

c)   ***The Hillary Clinton Effect: Stand by Your Man.*** In 1992, in a 60 Minutes interview with then Governor husband, Bill Clinton, Hillary publicly insulted the first lady of country music, Tammy Wynette, by using a popular song lyric to justify her position on sexual allegations against her husband. "I'm not sitting here like some little woman standing by my man like Tammy Wynette" she said in response to a question about allegations of her husband engaging in a 12-year extramarital affair with Gennifer Flowers.

Seven weeks later she said, "I suppose I could have stayed home and baked cookies and had teas" in response to questions about the appearance of conflicts of interest between her professional life and her husband's position as Governor of the State. Housewives around the country who took much pride in being domestic found these statements to be quite offensive and un-American.

d) *The Willy Wonka Effect* – In the 1971 movie, Willy Wonka & The Chocolate Factory, the young Julie Dawn Cole plays the spoiled Veruca Salt who makes demands of her wealthy father, Henry (played by Roy Mitchell Kinnear), and he gives her whatever she wants. In the movie, we never see where there is a mother.

> ➢ She was raised by a single father
> ➢ Men overly protect their daughters
> ➢ They don't allow their daughters to touch anything
> ➢ The father is highly chivalrous

e) **She doesn't cook:**

- A parent or hired help did it for her

f) **She doesn't like to clean:**

- She hires someone to do it for her

- She believes cleaning to be a sloppy, sweaty job.

- Her house stays clean because she limits activities that would create the need for maintenance.

g)   **She's not maternal:**

- She's awkward when she tries to interact with children.

- She lacks nurturing instincts. Caring for them does not come naturally.

- If he takes ill, she panics and calls for someone else to tend to him.

6.   **Sex is Complicated**

a)   **She doesn't like to kiss:**

- She feels it's sloppy and doesn't want to mess up her makeup.

b)   **She doesn't like kinky sex:**

- Hair pulling, face touching, etc. is out of the question as this will cause her to sweat.

- She worships her body, so she is very particular about what she does with it.

- She is not naturally submissive; kinky sex puts her in the position where she must be.

- She was possibly molested, raped, or sexually abused, which triggers traumatic occurrences. I remember having sex with a woman and she called me by her father's name. That's when I realized she'd probably been molested as a little girl.

c) **She doesn't like oral sex:**

- She doesn't like to look at his penis. To her it's an ugly, foreign object that she doesn't want to touch.

- When he climaxes, she doesn't want his sperm to touch her; she has him use towels to clean himself.

- She prefers to use a condom when having sex.

- She takes birth control (either the pill or the shot).

d) **She doesn't want to have sex for a long time:**

- She doesn't want to sweat

- She doesn't want to get dirty

e) **You must find clever ways to get her in the mood:**

- Atmosphere must be created

- She must be wined and dined

- She needs massages and/or baths

- She wants to have music playing

f) **There must be pillow talk:**

- Because she loves romance, the man must be willing to play the role.

- They discuss fantasies, dreams, and aspirations.

- He boosts her ego and compliments her, which turns her on.

- *This is different than his talk with Girl A because with Girl A he only discusses her physical appearance.

g) **She's sensual, not sexual:**

- *The American Beauty Effect* – In the 1999 hit movie, *American Beauty,* Kevin Spacey plays a sexually frustrated suburban father who becomes infatuated with his daughter's best friend (played by Mena Suvari). Her character, Angela Hayes, becomes the young fantasy of a man experiencing a middle-aged crisis. Once she realizes that he's interested, she teases him to no end, taunting him with visuals until he finally gets her alone and discovers an important secret (forgot to say, "Spoiler Alert", so I'll stop here).

- She likes romance – not sex
- She plays the role of a sex kitten

7. She Has a Disorder

a) She is obsessive-compulsive:

- She needs her house to stay clean

- She is extremely meticulous

  - If at a gas station pumping gas, she makes sure that the pump stops at an even number.

  - When grocery shopping, she pays the exact amount

b) She's ritualistic:

- All her bills are paid on time

- *The Rain Man Effect* – She must maintain her schedule

c) **She's always correcting people:**

- She's a grammar queen
- She enjoys teaching and instructing others

d) **She's seditty and self-righteous:**

- She displays signs of bitterness
- She's impatient and deceiving

e) **Social Isolation:**

- She is not transparent
- She wears a mask

f) **She's controlling:**

- She manipulates him

- She uses blackmail and extortion tactics to get what she wants. She threatens to tell his wife, family, etc. about their relationship.

- She makes him feel inadequate, uneducated, insignificant – like he's nothing without her

- She buys him things (food, clothes, furniture, etc.) to keep the upper hand

- so that when arguments ensue, she can say she bought it.

g) **She displays mental illness:**

- Depressive Disorder – Persistent feelings of sadness and worthlessness and a lack of desire to engage in formerly pleasurable activities.

- Emotional Detachment Disorder – often described as "emotional numbing" or dissociation, this disorder refers to an inability to connect with others on an emotional level, as well as a means of coping with anxiety by avoiding certain situations that trigger it.

- Aboulomania – also known as *analysis paralysis*, a person with this disorder displays extreme indecisiveness. The condition causes an individual to overthink a situation to the point of paralysis. No action is taken because a decision is never made.

Chapter Four:
The Interlude

You may be asking yourself, Why in the world is there an interlude in a book? Isn't that a component typically found in a song? Well, yes, it is. Interludes, or intermissions, can be found in both songs and musicals.

I remember when I was a child, I was marveled by MGM Musicals - ESPECIALLY The Ten Commandments and West Side Story (which had beautiful overtures). During these intermissions, I noticed two things: First, either the movie played the interlude or there was a live band in the musician's pit that played during the break increasing the overall experience. Second, some of the attendees would leave during this time to get snacks. While doing so, they'd discuss what they'd already seen in the production as well as make predictions for the outcome.

I never forgot how this made me feel. So once I became a musician, I understood the purpose of the interlude and how effective it could be if used appropriately. Those experiences helped me conclude that an interlude was exactly what this book needed. Why? One word - meditation.

Whether featured in music or plays, the interlude helps bring focus to what has already transpired. It's a time to reflect. I needed my readers to meditate on the message that's already been given, while preparing for what is about to unfold.

To assist with this process, I created a corresponding soundtrack, entitled Men's Chronicles that will provide a deeper sense of enlightenment and understanding.

Yes, this book is very opinionated, but there's a lot of truth as well, as I help you to see through the eyes of men, starting with me. You definitely see my transparency, to an almost embarrassing degree, but I figured, why lie? Who would it help?

There are many relationship experts out there. Whether you surf the internet, check Facebook or any other social media platform, you will stumble upon love gurus. Some are pretty good, give amazing advice, and have best-selling books, while others simply pander to their followers. You can spot them right away just by scrolling through their posts or videos. I noticed that some of the men side with women in almost ALL matters and even join in the male bashing. Personally, I find it disgusting and believe this technique to cause people to break up quicker. I refuse to side with a man simply because I'm a man; neither will I side with a woman just to build my audience.

I consider my approach like that of Apostle Paul, in that he didn't try to convince people by using lofty words and impressive wisdom. He too was quite transparent. To many, he appeared weak and timid because he didn't use big words or clever, persuasive speeches; but it was purposed. Why? Because he spoke to mixed audiences and understood it was necessary to be on level with whomever he encountered.

This book follows the same pattern. I understand that some will absolutely hate it due to their inability to understand it right now. Historically though, this has typically been the case. Some antiquated books were once shunned but became increasingly relevant as people changed and their lives evolved. To some, how I depict these women may come across as demeaning, as though I am bashing women. However, these depictions are everywhere. If you think about some of society's more popular television shows and movies, dating back 50 years, and even to present time, regardless of race, women have been perceived the way I classify them. Here are just a few examples:

Girl A

Lady Sings the Blues – In this 1972 classic, Diana Ross portrays Billie Holiday. Although she has a singing career (unconventional job), she is extremely sexual and accessible to her love interest (Billy Dee Williams).

Bonnie and Clyde – In the 1967 film, Bonnie (Faye Dunaway) is a small-town, uneducated girl, who is willing to perform illegal acts to please her man, Clyde (Warren Beatty).

Why Did I Get Married – In this 2007 drama, although she was married, Angela (Tasha Smith) was a typical ghetto girl freak.

Girl B

She-Devil – Ed Begley, Jr. plays Bob, the husband of a "plain Jane" in this 1989 comedy. He has an affair with a beautiful, rich, high-class author played by Meryl Streep, and ends up leaving his wife to be with her.

Basic Instinct – In this 1992 drama, Sharon Stone portrays a beautiful crime novelist who seduces a homicide detective to clear herself from being charged as a murder suspect.

Deliver Us from Eva – Eva (played by Gabrielle Union) is the eldest sister who has been responsible for her sisters since the death of their parents in this 2003 comedy. Men find it very difficult to approach her as she is very beautiful; has an intimidating demeanor; a good job; and is no-nonsense.

Girl C

Claudine – Although the title character, Claudine (Diahann Carroll) was a single mother of six in this 1974 classic, she possessed many Girl C traits (you will read about them in the next chapter).

One True Thing – In this 1998 movie, Meryl Streep played Kate, the undervalued matriarch, diagnosed with cancer. Like most Girl Cs, she was hardworking, loyal, and unappreciated.

Temptation – In Tyler Perry's 2013 blockbuster, Brice (Lance Gross) considered Judith (Jurnee Smollett-Bell) to be "the one". He was totally attracted to her beyond sexuality, as she loved him unconditionally.

Girl D

The Hand that Rocks the Cradle – Rebecca De Mornay portrays Peyton in this 1992 movie. She was beautiful, but dangerous with an axe to grind. She became obsessed with another woman's husband and wouldn't stop until she got what she wanted.

A Thin Line Between Love and Hate – In this 1996 film, Lynn Whitfied plays Brandi, a very beautiful and highly successful executive, who happened to be a bit unstable. Her mental issues were triggered with the very mention of love, and her relationship took a toll for the worst.

Acrimony – Melinda (Taraji P. Henson) becomes extremely bitter after feeling betrayed by her husband in this 2018 movie. This resentment leads her to go to some extremely desperate measures, indicative of Girl D.

Throughout the course of 2018's *Nappily Ever After*, the protagonist Violet Jones (Sanaa Lathan), exhibits qualities of each girl, captured by way of her ever-changing hairstyles.

Girl A – Blonde: During this stage of her life, she dressed a little trashy, wearing wigs, and short skirts, trying to get the attention of men. She was even willing to have a one-night stand.

Girl B – Weave: When she wore weave, she was so consumed about maintaining her appearance that she didn't allow herself to be fully vested in her relationship for fear that she would mess up her hair.

Girl C – Natural: It was during this time that she felt most like herself. She didn't feel the need to impress anyone. She's shaken her insecurities and was comfortable in her own skin.

Girl D – Bald: In what I like to call, *The Brittney Spears Effect*, Violet had a complete meltdown where she didn't know what to do. She couldn't come to terms with her life, much less how to process it, so she went to an extreme action of completing shaving her head.

But despite these various portrayals, keep in mind, just as nobody eats a box of chocolates and knows what's inside solely by looking at the exterior, neither will a man know a woman's true character just by looking at her appearance.

While conducting research for this book, I noticed a pattern with the men I polled and how the women they desired fit the system I've presented. I found three key factors that contributed in the type of woman a man desired, and they are his race; political affiliation and religious background.

Race

White, Black and Asian men usually want a woman who takes good care of her skin (no acne, bumps, scars, etc.) think Girl B, but is willing to negotiate if other parts of her body are pleasing to his eyes (Girl A). What I have noticed though is when a white man is attracted to a black woman, he usually prefers darker skin, while the black man is attracted to black women with lighter skin.

Politics

In an October 27, 2018 Politico Magazine article written by Justin Lehmiller, he noted, "Those who identified with being Republicans reported fantasizing about a range of activities that involved infidelity, orgies, and partner swapping (Girls A and D). Democrats fantasized more about BDSM activities". I realized that there was a thin line between preferences among these political parties.

Religion

In the church, sex is a rather taboo topic. Most teach that sex is not a subject for discussion unless it is in relation to marriage. The pulpit is the place where people receive sex therapy advice, which typically came in the form in being sentenced to Hell if it was discovered that you engaged in fornication or adultery. Most men that grew up with these values tended to desire a Girl C.

There is an obvious point that needs to be mentioned: Every woman will not fit my profile to a tee. For example, all Girl As don't come from a broken home; neither are they all single mothers or uneducated. Some have Girl B traits, and as you continue to read, you'll notice some Girl C traits as well.

And, if you hadn't noticed, I've categorized the women's qualities in what most men would consider "descending order". The Profile is comprised in a way to reflect what he desires most, which explains the reason(s) for his approach. Although he sees no future with Girl A, her sexuality appeals to him. Girl B may have some problems, but she's so beautiful to him that this characteristic must be placed at the top of the list; he won't see other issues until he gets to know her better.

As you read the next two chapters, you will see how Girls A and C are similar, just as Girls B and D are comparable in many ways.

Chapter Five:
Girl C (The Soulmate)

The year was 1981, and I was a teenager enjoying the effects of post puberty when I stumbled upon this beautiful girl at our new church. Her smile was captivating, her face was smooth, her teeth were white, and her laugh was infectious. Whenever she sat next to me, I would shake with nervousness, perspire and my heart would beat fast. I couldn't understand why no other girl did this to me. I then realized that I was "Twitter pated", yep that's right twitter pated – a word I had just discovered while Watching a VHS copy of Walt Disney's animated movie, *Bambi*. It's that flighty exciting feeling you get when you see the object of your affection. I would get completely enamored with her.

As time went on, we started going "steady" (keep in mind, this is 1981). Anyway, whenever we were alone and held hands, nothing on my body would move but my heart; whenever I embraced her, my hands always rested on her back, never below the waistline. There was no sneaking in bedroom windows or necking in the backseat of my parents' car in some park at night. What was it about this girl that made me feel a need to respect and protect her? I realized that I had fallen in love for the first time and didn't know the course that was being set was about to last for years to come – like a drug addict's FIRST high. I spent years trying to recapture that feeling.

I have realized that Girl Cs are "Home Grown", and just like the rejected bride in the Eddie Murphy movie,

Coming to America, they are groomed from birth. In the movie, Prince Akeem (Eddie Murphy) was willing to lose his chance to sit on the throne just to be with Lisa McDowell (Shari Headley), for he loved her unconditionally and nothing else mattered to him. Although Cleo McDowell (John Amos) was rich, his daughter Lisa was meeker, and focused her time on the poor.

Some of you who are Girl Cs will read the following profile and say, "Surely this is not me". I get it, maybe it's not you. But answer this question honestly, "Do you REALLY know what your man sees in you"? If you truly understood that he loves you for your heart, you wouldn't ask him how he feels about your body, much less asking a question such as, "Does this dress make my butt look big?" I present to you, Girl C...

The Profile – referred to as "The Soulmate", this is the woman that he can't live without. He may lovingly call her, *Wifey*, because he knows his life isn't the same without her. This is the woman that he would be willing to give up everything for because she is his difference maker.

1. She's the One

   a) She doesn't ask him for anything but his time:

      - She's a giver. It's in her nature to give because she was raised to be that way.

   b) She remembers his words:

      - Flattery for him – After conducting a poll among men, I discovered that for many men, this quality is a must.

      - A huge sign of respect

   c) She edifies him:

      - She always expresses how proud she is of him, which is vital because there is a little boy inside of every man that needs that praise and validation from who he loves most.

      - He respects her thoughts and opinions.

      - She helps him execute his goals and dreams.

      - *The Minister Jones Effect – She's cunning and knows how to get his attention.*

- I remember one day, my then wife wanted to speak to me. She'd been trying to get my attention before, but to no avail. This time, she made an unusual request – she requested that I meet her in my full clergy attire (collar, rope, cross, and black suit) as she wanted to speak with Minister Jones. I didn't understand until she explained that whenever Minister Jones appeared, she received results. So, she arrived at my office at 7pm and made me give her marital counseling. As her counselor, I was bound to tell her the truth about everything.

d) **He trusts her with all that he has:**

- Family

  ➢ She has proven that her love and loyalty to him and anything attached to him is genuine.

- Feelings

  ➢ There is a little boy inside of all men. He feels comfortable being vulnerable with her about everything including his past.
  ➢ He allows her to see every side of him

- o Silliness
- o Sadness
- o Seriousness

- Finances

  - ➢ If they don't have joint accounts, he has given her his account numbers and passwords.

- Future

  - ➢ He seeks her advice and guidance in all that he desires to do because he wants her to be part of it.

e) She's a nurturer:

- During my married years, my wife taught me so many valuable lessons. I remember volunteering my time to play the organ for a church on Sunday nights, and one night a familiar musician came to visit. The Pastor was so overtaken by this man's presence that he spent a considerable amount of time in his opening address praising the musician. I was in no way offended, for I too jumped on the bandwagon in honest adoration. The Pastor then began to speak of this gentleman as if he was the greatest and ONLY musician the church ever had. My heart sank because he had never once said my name over the pulpit in the years I'd been assisting. I was so hurt that I quickly left for fear of crying publicly. I didn't know why it hurt me so, but it did, to my very core. My wife stayed home that evening, so when I got home, I found her watching TV in the bedroom. I kneeled at the bedside and put my head in her lap, cried and told her what happened. In my utter brokenness, she began to console and edify me. Most men can tell you a story like this that he will remember all his life about his Girl C.

f) She cares about his total well-being:

- There isn't one aspect of his life that she ignores. It is her joy to please him. She tends to him spiritually, physically, and financially.

g) He's physically attracted to her:

- He doesn't see her physically as he does other women (Girl A, B and D). He doesn't lust after her. His desire for her is beyond physical; he has a true, unconditional connection with her.

- During sex, he's delicate and gentle with her.

- He will nurse her when she's sick.

- In pregnancy, he will rub her belly.

- He compliments her despite how she looks esthetically because he only sees her beauty.

2. She Loves Him Unconditionally

a) She's his ride or die:

- *The Edith Bunker Effect* – She protects and/or defends him at all cost.

- She is an honest woman who doesn't care to lie, but will embellish for his sake.

b) Her mission is to please him by any means necessary:

- manicures
- pedicures
- haircuts
- massages
- She writes him love letters and leaves them in places she knows he will find them.

c) **She's his personal nurse:**

- She takes care of him when he's sick
- She knows most recipes for holistic remedies.

d) **She prays for him:**

- They once prayed together, but when the sex stopped, so did his desire to pray with her.

e) **She doesn't mind being the breadwinner:**

- If he loses his job, she will do whatever is necessary to keep things together.

f) **She gives him sex whenever he asks for it:**

- It may be boring to her
- She may not want it
- She's spiritual and was raised to never deny him.

g) **Even after infidelity, she's willing to stay with him:**

- She has invested everything in this man
- She won't give him up without a fight

3. **She's Introduced to His Circle**

a) **He married his mom:**

- Unlike the other women, she's someone he can be proud of because she's comparable to his mother.

b) **She has things in common with his mother:**

- He chose her because she puts him in a nostalgic place. She reminds him of good times – how things used to be.

c) **She can have a conversation that won't embarrass him:**

- She may not be college educated, but she has a keen sense of learning people.

- She walks in discernment

- She's wise

- She's kindhearted, which empowers him.

d) **She's taken to company picnics:**

- If he's showing her off, he's decided that she's the one.

e) **She's invited to family reunions:**

- Usually at this stage, they are engaged.

f) **She accompanies him to church services:**

- Their spiritual life is very important to them individually, so they need to see how they worship corporately.

g) **They go on dates with his married friends:**

- A bond must be built with their best friends.

- Approval of mate selection from best friends is sometimes more meaningful than that of the family because many times friends know more than family.

4. **She's Domestic**

a) **She caters to him:**

- She will do whatever he asks, which can sometime be at the cost of her personal convictions.

b) **She keeps his life organized:**

- Balances books
- Sets doctors' appointments; makes sure he goes
- Pays bills

- Makes dollars stretch (good with budget)

c) **She has chef qualities:**

- She was taught by a maternal figure (mother, grandmother, aunt) how to cook at an early age.

- She knows her kitchen better than anybody.

- Even when the cupboard is bare, she can make something out of nothing.

- There is no cultural dish that she can't cook.

- She watches cooking shows

- Her kitchen is a library for cooking magazines.

- As they age, she becomes more health conscious.

- She makes sure that he eats well

d) *The Soccer Mom Effect – She takes care of his children:*

- She sacrifices her comforts for theirs

- She attends their school events

- She helps with homework

- She makes sure they are well-groomed

- She knows the children's friends and parents

- She knows all their favorites

    - Foods
    - Movies
    - Songs
    - Colors

e) **She's a homemaker:**

- She subscribes to home and garden magazine.

- Her home is her office and she is the CEO.

- She designates duties for all family members and micromanages them well (See Chapter 7).

- She's resourceful and always has a backup plan

    - Money
    - Food
    - Batteries

- Her home is like a shelter. She always buys items for others because she knows at any given moment, she may be responsible for someone else's well-being

f) His immediate family loves her:

- They thank her for marrying him

- She always respects his mother

- She's always asking about his family

- She will visit his parents with or without him

- Even after marriage dissolves, she'll always be considered part of the family.

g) She's very hospitable:

- She's a gracious host
- She's capable of entertaining guests
- She knows how to create ambiance for the room

5. She's A Plain Jane

a) She's pretty at first, but then becomes plain:

- She's not high maintenance.

- *The New Toy Effect* – He no longer sees her as being pretty because she doesn't measure up to the other women he encounters on a regular basis.

b) **She stopped trying to look pleasing to him:**

- She has let herself go.

- She used to take the time to make herself up, but with time and an increase in responsibilities she stopped.

c) **She doesn't buy trendy clothes:**

- She normally wears jeans and t-shirts.

- She dresses for comfort, not to impress.

d) **They don't go out much:**

- He's bored with her

- She's practical and doesn't see the need to spend money when she can cook at home. She feels they can allocate that money elsewhere.

e) **She's usually alone in the house – even when he's home:**

- Housework consumes her time

- She's nonchalant about her lifestyle

- She doesn't need the finer things in life. She appreciates it if received but doesn't require it.

- Rarely discusses goals and dreams because even if she brings them up, they are ignored

f) **She's doe-witted:**

- She has no sense of style or personality.

g) **They don't share interests anymore:**

- They once had all things in common, but like all things they have come to an end.

- What they once found appealing about each other now drives them up a wall.

6. **She Suspects There Are Others**

a) *The Della B Effect* – She stopped nagging about there being others and accepted it, even to the point of helping them.

b) **She stops giving him sex (or gives test sex):**

- She needs to know if her intuition is right. I was in counseling with a man who had indeed cheated on his wife one night. When he got home, he took a shower and got into bed with her. She had already suspected he was a cheater, plus showering before bed was not his typical routine. He told me that he had climaxed with the other woman, which rendered him too weak for another round of sex with his wife. She knew this trait about him and then she went outside of their routine by asking him for sex. He, knowing that this was merely "test sex", mustered up enough strength and was surprisingly able to endure until he climaxed once more. He told me it was the hardest thing he ever had to do, but he was willing to go through it to try and salvage their relationship.

c)   **She checks his devices:**

- Her fear is discovering the truth, so initially she's reluctant to check his devices, but she finds evidence in the first place she looks.

d)   **She smells his body/clothes:**

- The Body Cavity Search

➢ She checks for odors and fragrances

➢ Checks his clothes for lipstick

➢ Sniffs his underwear

➢ *The Bar Stool Test of Pheromones* – I remember reading a study done on a bachelor where they sent him to a bar to see how many women would be attracted to him as he sat alone; hardly any women approached him. They then sprayed pheromones on him that same night and had him reenter the bar. It was the smell of other women in the pheromones. Before you knew it, several women who'd previously ignored him, stopped and turned around to sit with him.

e) **She asks questions to trap him:**

- She's subtle in her questioning.

- If he's cheating, she wants to know if he loves her.

- Because he knows her thought pattern, he purposely starts fights so he can leave the house.

f)   She's slow to confront the other women:

- Once it gets out of control and creates deep issues within the marriage, she will react.

g)   As a last resort, she will hire a private investigator:

- She is not in to embarrass him, she simply wants closure, so she can officially move on.

7.   The Romance Has Left

a)   They don't kiss anymore unless it's during sex:

- Kissing is attached to the heart

b)   They don't show public displays of affection:

- Their love is fading, so like kissing, public displays of affection communicate that all things are well within the relationship.

c)   Personal dates no longer exist:

- They only go out with children or extended family.

d)   When they go out, it's only to buffet or family-style restaurants:

- He doesn't take her to expensive restaurants.

- If he's cheating, he's saving his body, time and money for someone else.

e) **There is no communication:**

- Conversation is only to take care of business.

  - ➤ House
  - ➤ Children
  - ➤ Church

f) **They have a boring sex life:**

- If it happens at all, it's because he wants it, and in some cases, he forces it.

- She shows signs of loneliness and depression.

g) *The "TAP OUT" Effect* – **She is finished with the relationship:**

- They sleep in separate beds or rooms.

- She's falling out of love and will eventually become mute with him.

- If she cheats on him, he wants to know who's better.

- Prior to my marriage ending, I remember taking a nap on the couch one evening while watching my favorite show. The next night, I turned on the show and after a while, I fell asleep again on the couch. This continued for about two weeks straight until that series' season ended. I then decided to go lay in our bed, and to my surprise, my wife turned to me and asked, "What are you doing? Your bed is in the living room". You see, I didn't realize that I was giving her two weeks to "tap out" – that was all it took. I spent a good six months on that couch until we finally separated.

- *The Quincy Jones Effect* – While he was working on the movie, The Color Purple, there was a continuous strain on the relationship between he and his wife. By the time he returned home, she was gone because she'd tapped out!

Chapter Six:
Girl D (Fatal Attraction)

I remember sitting among the clergy one Sunday morning and caught the eye of a beautiful woman staring at me. I didn't know what to make of it, and it really didn't matter much because I was single and was hoping and praying that she was too. This went on for a couple weeks until I finally built up enough nerve to ask her out. She said yes and before you knew it, we were going out every day. You pretty much found us everywhere – in clothing stores, restaurants, parks and even her house.

One day I called to tell her I thought it was just too much and that we needed to slow down. Out of nowhere she began to scream on her cellphone, all while driving to my place to confront me. It was at that moment I realized that she was the one dictating this relationship. She started doing background checks on me and calling former employers. She even used some Jedi Mind Trick on me to keep me hen pecked until one day I finally broke free and ran for my life.

It occurred to me that I had dated this woman before in other cities. All of them used sugar and baited me in, exemplified Girl B traits at first and then went for the kill. It reminded me of a time I saw Creationist Kent Hovind use a box of d-CON rat poison to demonstrate how easy it was to destroy life. The ingredients on the box showed 0.005% poison and 99.995% good food. I've always been a mild-mannered man and these women used that fact to their advantage to draw me into the .005%. One would just faint in front of my friends and family; another would go into an anger tantrum in public to embarrass me; another would try to degrade me intellectually because she had several college degrees; yet another used sex to control me.

When I finally settled down and got married, one of them insisted that I divorce my wife and return to her or else. In the 1987 movie, *Fatal Attraction*, Glenn Close plays the role of a book editor named Alex, who falls in loves with lawyer Dan Gallagher (played by Michael Douglas) after sleeping together. He liked her as well, however, he couldn't be with her because he was married and tried to break free of her. She didn't take the breakup well; in fact, she became obsessed with him. This brings me to my point. Girl D wants to be loved. She wants to do good, but evil is present. This evil is locked up in the corners of her mind, coming out to play when triggered...possibly due to a childhood trauma or PTSD that wasn't managed. I introduce you to, Girl D...

The Profile – She truly is a "Fatal Attraction". This is the woman that may be beautiful like "The Mistress" but his enjoyment is connected to the sexual domination he experiences with her. Although she may be mentally unstable, for him, the risk is well worth the reward.

1. She's A Professional Woman

    a) **She has a managerial role (Partner/CEO/Business Owner):**

    - Any other position belittles her
    - She comes from a middle/upper class home

    b) **She's educated:**

    - She attended the best schools and got perfect grades
    - She has college degrees
    - See Girl B

    c) **She doesn't have children:**

    - If she does, she is not the primary caretaker
    - She's not very nurturing
    - See Girl B

    d) **She's high-class and only associates with high-class individuals:**

    - She doesn't have many friends
    - She thinks her business associates are enough
    - In some cases, she feels her business associates are her friends

    e) **She enjoys the finer things in life:**

- She only eats at the best restaurants
- She only stays at 5-star hotels
- She wears expensive jewelry

f) **She has investments:**

- Her parents taught her the world of investments

- She realized that to blend in with "her crowd", she had to be like them

- She subscribes to Wall Street Journal; watches stock market reports and CNBC

g) **She's no-nonsense (very serious):**

- Her parent(s) was strict yet highly successful

- She's influenced by her industry

2. **She's Image Conscious**

a) **She's very beautiful:**

- She's a perfect 10
- He's smitten by her

b) **She always wears makeup:**

- She tried it as a teenager, and now can't live without it

- Makeup is part of her mask she hides behind

- When no makeup is applied, you can see the marks/scars she's trying to hide

c) **She wears designer originals:**

- Whether or not she got the things she wanted as a child didn't stop her from wanting and pursuing them

- Even when she couldn't afford it, she knew that image would sustain quality friends and help her climb the corporate ladder

d) **Most of her social media pics are of herself:**

- She's self-absorbed
- She's always careful how the world perceives her
- Image is everything to her, so every pic is carefully chosen

e) **She's only seen with high class people:**

- At times, she will choose people she feels are low-class to be around because their status makes her feel better about herself

f) **She only owns the best:**

- All her assets say she's wealthy – even if she's not

g) **She travels because of perceived status:**

- She always travels first class
- She will book flights to exotic places just to say she's gone

3. **Sexually Dominating**

a) **She's hypersexual (nymphomaniac):**

- She's a paraphilia (has fetishes)
- She's into cybersex

b) **She likes to experiment with sex:**

- Positions
- Length of time
- Porn emulations (soft vs. hardcore)
- Polyamory – a mutual agreement to be romantically involved with multiple partners

c) **She prefers spontaneous and risky sex:**

- Public places
- Car
- Mile High Club
- Alley
- Park
- Church
- Bathroom

d) She prefers erotic language:

- For her "dirty talk" is the implementation of pornographic lingo

e) She enjoys role play (the outfits are a turn-on):

- Nurse
- Nun
- Priest
- Teachers

f) They have lots of sex videos:

- She enjoys seeing what she did to him
- She wants to be his sole pleasure

g) She's into BDSM:

- Cuckoldress

4. She's Extremely Private

a) She's lonely:

- *The Hulk Effect – "You won't like me when I'm angry".* She's had so many disappointments with people that being alone is safe for her

- In the movie, Thin Line Between Love and Hate, she says, "Don't tell me you love me" because she knows what she's capable of once enticed or provoked.

b)   **Her co-workers don't know about him:**

- Her job is important to her. That's where her "other personality" lives. Formerly known as Multiple Personality Disorder, DID or Dissociative Identity Disorder, is a mental disorder that is characterized by at least two distinct and relatively enduring personality traits. Girl D is a carrier. People with this sickness tend to forget certain events, beyond "ordinary" forgetfulness. Professionals believe the cause to be childhood trauma or PTSD and they've discovered this in about 90% of cases. When left untreated, it gets worse. It is diagnosed about six times more often in females than in males. Surprisingly, she could have worked on her job for years and her coworkers not see it…only those who are in close relation with her (family or lovers).

c)   **She has very little contact with her family:**

- She doesn't get along with her parents or siblings because she feels as though she doesn't belong

d) **She might've had a name change:**

- She may have had to hide from an ex or is escaping from questionable people.

e) **She's religious...who'd would've thought:**

- She goes to church because she feels convicted (The Sopranos).

- She knows she can find other men to prey on (Get Out).

f) **She has a routine to keep people from suspecting her behavior:**

- Due to her paranoia, she feels that someone is always watching her

g) **She won't discuss parts of her past (secret life):**

- She doesn't want to lose him
- She is embarrassed about her past

5. **She's Controlling**

a) **She buys him things:**

- This is her way of grooming him
- He is becoming the fatted calf
- He is becoming Girl B

b) **She dictates his mannerisms and behaviors:**

- *The Slave Master Effect* – She tries to recreate him by erasing him

c) **She threatens him (veiled or overt):**

- She cuts off his privileges

  - ➤ Sexual
  - ➤ Financial

- She says she will hurt herself

d) **She belittles him:**

- She makes public scenes to embarrass him

- She insults his ego. She makes him feel bad because she makes more money than he does

e) **She separates him from his family and friends:**

- This is part of her attempt to recreate him. She strips him and must separate him from everyone else for it to be effective

- She doesn't know how to be alone

f) **She's manipulative:**

- She says or does whatever is necessary to get her way

    ➢ Cries
    ➢ Lies

- She controls sexual activity

    ➢ Frequency
    ➢ Times/Days
    ➢ Positions

g) **She excessively calls and texts:**

- She's jealous and needs to know his every move

6. She is Mentally Unstable

a) **She's either overly spoiled or totally ignored:** In the 1962 psychological thriller-horror film, "What Ever Happened to Baby Jane", Jane Hudson (Bette Davis) was a child actress who loved the limelight, for her father spoiled her. Her sister, Blanche (Joan Crawford), was also a former child actress but was harshly treated by her father and always blamed for upsetting her sister Jane. Stuck living together in a mansion in old Hollywood, Blanche plots to get even with Jane for the car crash that left her crippled years earlier. In the movie, Blanche was depicted as caring and loving to all, even though this trauma happened to her...this is the Girl D that I recognized. In my dealings with her, she was ignored in life; she was kind, but always plotting.

b) *The Functioning Alcoholic Effect* – **Many can't see that she has a dysfunction because she's able to hide it.** I'd heard about functioning alcoholics, but never really met one until I started to seriously date. I had a girlfriend who I knew drank a lot because of the smell of her skin and clothes, but she seemed normal. Over time, I noticed discolorations in her skin and nails, slurred speech, clumsiness, rotting teeth, hair falling out and self-inflicted isolation. Yet, she woke up sober every morning, was always on time for work, did her eight hours and socialized like everybody else. After we broke up, I was told she lost everything due to this sickness, and the fact that it had not been dealt with early.

Sometimes, loved ones don't find out Girl D is a high functioning alcoholic until after an alcohol-related accident or a sickness.

c) **She exhibits signs of Bipolar Disorder:**

- Manic Depression
- Anxiety Attacks
- High Sex Drive

- Insomnia
- Anger
- Euphoria
- Crying
- Self-harm

d) Obsessive Compulsive Disorder (OCD):

- See Girl B for explanation

e) She's a Stalker:

- Paranoia
- Jealousy

f) She's Abusive:

- Physically
- Mentally
- Emotionally

g) She's Narcissistic:

- She's self-righteous and exaggerates

- She has sociopathic traits

7. She's A Drama Queen

a) She's mean to those she feels are beneath her (service workers):

- She's mimicking the behavior she saw her parents display

- Her industry is fast-paced, so she's not very patient or meek.

- She's short-tempered

b) **Never cancel on her:**

- She holds a double standard as it pertains to timeliness.

c) **She's always the victim:**

- "Nobody Likes Me Mentality"

- She reverts to her childhood. She becomes that little girl again. Something has triggered her repressed memories.

- *The Michael Jackson Effect* – Her childhood was stolen.

d) **She hates other women:**

- She never thought she was pretty enough in school

- She possibly lost an ex due to an affair

- *The Single White Female Effect – She sees them as a threat.* In this 1992 movie, Hedra Carlson (played by Jennifer Jason Leigh) moves in

- with Allison Jones (played by Bridget Fonda). Hedra becomes jealous of Allison and her relationship, and then grows hostile and violent to eliminate what she believes to be her competition.

e) **She throws temper tantrums when she doesn't get her way:**

- The little girl is always there waiting to make her appearance.

f) **She is over the top when displaying her emotions:**

- She can be very calm and enduring until provoked. Then she goes from 0 to 100.

g) **She's extremely picky:**

- Food
- Clothes

Chapter Seven:
The Renewed Mind

Up to this point, I have described the various types of women that men desire. There was no judgment of their behaviors - simply explanations of the traits and characteristics that these women possess. Although I advised against trying to identify yourself as one of the women, whether or not you admit it aloud, you have probably spent a great deal of time self-diagnosing.

So, I want to give you a resolve. If, in fact, you believe that you have correctly identified yourself and are unhappy with the result, this final chapter will teach you how to transition into the woman you want to become...and it all starts with a renewed mind.

A Renewed Mind

And be not conformed to this world: but be ye transformed by the renewing of your mind, that ye may prove what is that good, and acceptable, and perfect, will of God. – Romans 12:2 KJV

Romans Chapter 12 is a staple in the Pentecostal church. I'm sure I've heard hundreds of sermons prepared from this text and most Christians can at least quote verse 1 and 2 without having to Google. The reason I'm bringing this up and have chosen this particular text to end this book is due to two words that King James Version uses, "Transformed and Renewing". The women I feature in this Volume of the Men's Chronicles need a crash course in this most magnificent Pauline letter. The New International Version (NIV) brings out the text even clearer:

"Don't copy the behavior and customs of this world, but let God transform you into a new person by changing the way you think. Then you will learn to know God's will for you, which is good and pleasing and perfect."

Many women fail to see how sex appeal and beauty may attract but not always KEEP a man. In the sitcom series Gilligan's Island, Ginger and Mary Ann were the reason most little boys (like me) even watched that show. Tina Louise played Ginger Grant, the glamorous movie star, while Dawn Wells played Mary Ann, an innocent country farm girl from Kansas. Every boy my age was glued to the television whenever Ginger would show up in a scene; she was a fox and she would always seduce the men on the Island to get them to do what she wanted. The issue with her though was that she was Girl B – high maintenance and you would always lose her to the highest bidder.

Mary Ann was kind of complex if you really examined her closely but in reality, she would be most men's choice. She was your stereotypical farmer's daughter, wholesome but would rock your world around 2am when the farm was asleep. She spoke like a Girl C but dressed like a Girl A. Daisy Duke (Catherine Bach) from the TV Show Dukes of Hazzard would be likened to Mary Ann, as well as Elly May Clampett (Donna Douglas) of The Beverly Hillbillies.

Then there's Janet Wood (Joyce DeWitt) and Chrissy
Snow (Suzanne Somers) of the TV show Three's
Company. Janet was a lovable honest, down-to-earth
florist and Chrissy was your stereotypical ditzy blonde.
Most men (and us boys) in the 70's watched that show
and saw these women in the same way. Chrissy was
our one-night stand, but Janet was our forever girl.

Janet spoke to the little boy in us, she was Mom, she
was that 5th grade teacher I had a crush on, and she
was our high school sweetheart all in one. Janet was
too perfect for most though as she didn't take risks or
live on the edge and in shaky times, men would have
cheated on her with Chrissy (Girl A). The sad thing
about Chrissy is that her sex appeal is all most men
saw in her – a temporary fix. Once they were done with
her, they'd run back home to Janet.

Yeah, there was something about Jeannie (Barbara
Eden) in the bottle that drove men wild, and it had
nothing to do with her ability to grant wishes; it was
the way she loved and protected Captain Tony Nelson
(Larry Hagman). She, like Edith Bunker (Jean
Stapleton) of All in the Famly, was very naive but
trustworthy. They both were Girl Cs but the only
difference between the two was public sex appeal.

Edith Bunker was considered less attractive, but most
men knew they needed her and just desired Jeannie.
On the All in the Family episode entitled, "The Stivics
Go West", Mike and Gloria move to California to start a
new life. In the closing scene, Archie hugs them
goodbye, shuts the door and sits in his favorite
chair. He asks Edith to get him a beer out of the

refrigerator and while she's in the kitchen, he pulls out of his pocket a handkerchief and starts to cry. This was one of those rare moments when America saw a bigoted man's heart. Edith entered the room to see him crying and immediately retreats to the kitchen. Why? Because she knew that Archie was a prideful man who never allowed her to see him so vulnerable; she knew to give him that time alone. Before she reenters the room, she loudly announces that she's coming with his beer, which gives him time to straighten himself out.

Jeannie had chances with many men. She evolved during the series and the writers of the show even allowed Tony to eventually marry her. Other men desired Jeannie though and as you read in my Girl A & B analogies, you see how his own best friend (Captain Roger Healey) stole her in the episode entitled "The Richest Astronaut in the Whole Wide World).

I can find so many scenarios in Hollywood where producers pushed these contrasts of women on us to fight over, for it kept us engaged. Some of the actresses even played their own antithesis through special camera effects. Jean Stapleton played Edith Bunker and the grumpy girlfriend of a local butcher who was in love with Edith by the name of "Judith" (IMDB). Barbara Eden played Jeannie and an evil fraternal twin sister in the 2nd season, also named "Jeannie" wearing a brunette wig. Lastly, on the TV series, Bewitched, we see the loyal Samantha Stevens (Elizabeth Montgomery) who is periodically visited by her flirtatious cousin Serena, also played by Elizabeth Montgomery. Men surely had the hots for Serena (Girl D), but it was Samantha's shoulder in whom all men cried on. Just ask both Darrins, and they'll tell you.

Mankind has a bad habit of developing carbon copies of someone else's madness. Sure, emulation is said to be the greatest form of flattery, but not when you are copying someone's sociopathic or abusive behavior. Many believe they have no choice as it pertains to their future. They believe that because their parents did something, they must do it too. Whether it's the job they work, the habits they develop, and even the people they date, the belief is, "Because my parents did it this way, I must repeat the same pattern".

In many church circles, they call these generational curses, but I personally don't believe in them. I believe that people have become overly spiritual in teaching this, while dismissing the art of copying and not taking the time to study gene mirroring, which is not a curse, but something that is physiologically passed down. Both Numbers 14:18 and Exodus 20:5 tells us that God will not ignore the guilty and that He will punish the children until the third and fourth generations all for the sins of the fathers. We then see in Deuteronomy 24:16 and Ezekiel 18:19-20 how God then reverses this decision by saying, "What? you ask. 'Doesn't the child pay for the parent's sins?' No! For if the child does what is just and right and keeps my decrees, that child will surely live".

I believe a person reaps what he sows, and the Laws of Nature can be quite reliable. Having sex with a person who is known to have HIV can greatly increase your chances of contracting the same virus. This is not a curse; this is a recompense of a natural law. Touch a hot stove and you WILL get burned. God didn't do this, nor did Satan, you did this. Notwithstanding,

Galatians 3:10 speaks of the book of the Law and that those who rely on "works" of the law are under a curse.

The truth was hidden from the women in this book, for knowing this truth, would have set them free (John 8:32). For others, they purposely rejected this truth; in bible times God destroyed His people for rejecting knowledge (Hosea 4:6). Fast forward to today...there is no condemnation for those who are in Christ Jesus, PERIOD! Why him though? Because there's another law we tend to forget, which is the Law of the Spirit of Life. It sets you free in this same Christ from that earlier law we mentioned, "Law of Sin and Death". Finally, Christ redeemed you from the curse of the law by becoming a curse for you. How did he do that? He hung on a tree (Galatians 3:13).

My point in all of this is to say, why would God insist you transform by changing your mind if He put you under a generational curse? What about all these families who seem to have the same traits, attributes, dysfunctions and diseases, you ask? That's a good question. My answer: Deoxyribonucleic acid (DNA), is self-replicating and is the carrier of genetic information. Pretty much, it is a gift to you from your parents.

There's a thin line between inheritance and heredity. When someone says, "You act just like your daddy.", that's not a curse. It represents a passed down trait and you had no say in the matter. If your father was an abusive man, and you realize that you too are abusive, you are either choosing to harm someone or you have allowed Satan to sift you as wheat. So, you feel a burning desire to do this? You feel trapped in a social box? Well, look closely…the box is made from breakable glass. When I was in grammar school, there was a sign under the encased fire extinguisher that read, "In Case of Fire, Break Glass". Ladies, your ceilings with men are made of glass, and not as thick as you may think – you must simply adjust your mind to believe you can break it!

From the Beginning

Since the creation, a woman has been the most influential person in a man's life. When the serpent was looking for someone to deceive, he knew it would be better to target Eve, and not solely because she was the weaker vessel. He targeted her because he knew that if he could trick her, she would get Adam. A man will do anything for the woman he loves (or lusts). Adam was one with Eve and he purposely gave up paradise for her by committing the ultimate sin in the Garden.

I remember when I was coming up, if a salesman would ring the bell or call on the phone, he would ask, "Is the woman of the house available?" Why? He understood the cliché to be true, Happy Wife, Happy Life. In other words, he knew that if the woman wanted what he was offering, the man wouldn't be an issue because she had the power of persuasion.

The Women of the Bible

The point of my bringing up the creation, as with the other women of the bible is to demonstrate that as Ecclesiastes 1:9 says, "there's nothing new under the sun". I may have labeled them Girls A – D, but these women show up in many areas in scripture. The bible seems to portray women as property or at best, second class citizens. I'm reminded of the sermons about the woman who was raped all night long by evil men and was left on the doorstep dead, she was then cut into twelve pieces and her body parts were delivered to the tribes of Israel (Judges 19). There was also Jacob's daughter Dinah who was minding her own business and allegedly raped by Shechem, a Hivite Prince, who then fell for her and asked for her hand in marriage (Genesis 34).

However, when you take a closer look, you'll notice a few of these women had their way with their respective men. Think about Tamar who played the harlot just to have an offspring in the line of Judah. How did she accomplish this? By holding Judah's staff, seal and chord hostage as ransom to prove he was the father of her baby. Esther knew King Ahasuerus was interested in her, so she used her beauty to her advantage to ultimately become queen and save her people. David was so infatuated with Bathsheba that he had her husband (who was a soldier in his army) killed just so he could be with her. Jezebel was married to a man that she walked all over. She used her power to not only kill prophets, but also to make Israel worship Baal.

As you can see, past or present, women are equipped to have their way with a man. There is more than one way to make this happen. Whether you decide to use your looks or prowess, the methodology starts with the mindset.

The Mind of...

Listed below are biblical women categorized by my modern-day criteria. The idea is to further expound on the fact that these behaviors and mindsets have always existed, and that there are direct parallels between today's woman and the woman of yesteryear.

Woman at the Well – Girl A

This woman met Jesus at the well and was very hospitable; she served him as requested. When Jesus asked where her husband was, she responded that she didn't have one. Jesus told her that she was right because she'd had several, and none of them belonged to her.

I was working in a factory one year and while on my lunch break my co-worker talked about how easy church girls were. He said he was dating a girl who was very spiritual but always vulnerable around him. One day he stopped by the church during a revival, he saw his girl in the church jumping and shouting and speaking in tongues. He walked over to the door, she saw him, quickly grabbed her purse, got in his car and he drove her to the nearest hotel for sex.

Moral of the Story: Girl As may know Jesus, but they struggle to overcome temptation.

Delilah – Girl B

Delilah was a Philistine woman, who had caught the attention of Samson, an Israelite warrior. She was "forbidden fruit" and he knew it, yet because of his love/lust for her, he got entangled with her and exposed his secret, which ultimately killed him.

I dated a woman who was drop dead gorgeous, from top to bottom and would have won any modeling and beauty contest. She was very educated, well-spoken and managed her money well. She had an infectious laugh a dazzling smile and could join any subject in the room. So, what was her problem? Apparently, I was. I wasn't perfect enough and she treated me more like her son than she did her man. At home she cooked and cleaned for me and offered up her body, but in public, she would humiliate me. When the chips were down, like Delilah, she turned on me. Those who were trying to destroy my character, turned to her for help, and before it all was over, I realized that I had been to a female barbershop.

Moral of the Story: Girl Bs may appear sweet on the outside, but they can be bitter once you get involved with them.

Sarah – Girl C
Sarah knew Abraham better than anybody. She knew what made him tick and she knew that addressing him as "lord" would turn things in her favor every time; reciprocity would then follow. As 1 Peter 3:7 says, "…. treat your wife with understanding as you live together. She may be weaker than you are, but she is your equal partner in God's gift of new life".

In the profile of Girl C in this book, I briefly mentioned how my wife cunningly got my attention by asking me to speak to "Minister Jones". As Minister, or Elder Jones in some circles, people in religious organizations perceived me to be an important man, especially when I would put on my vestment. We lived in a predominantly Hispanic neighborhood called Humboldt

Park in Chicago and whenever they saw me with the collar on, they referred to me as "Father". My wife noticed that I walked and talked differently when in full regalia and I transformed into this great servant of the people. She knew that if she addressed me as others did, that I would tend to her needs at home, for my wife found a way to tap into my identity.

Moral of the Story: Girl Cs know how to use their humility to get to the heart of their man.

Potiphar's Wife – Girl D
This was a deceitful woman. She wanted to have her way with Joseph, and when he refused her, she screamed rape, and had him falsely imprisoned.

I have learned that some women get angry when you stand for righteousness. I had a girlfriend who would visit me daily. Before long, she was spending nights at my house. Next thing I knew, she had clothes in my closet. When I brought it to her attention that biblically, we were doing things the wrong way, she became very angry and began to lash out.

Moral of the Story: Girl Ds are willing to sacrifice their dignity to get what they want.

The Ruth and Boaz Effect

I was reading Proverbs 6 one day and it reinforced the notion even more that the way that women act and the way that men perceive them is nothing new. In verse 20, there are instructions to a son that he must hear from his father regarding women. He said, "It will keep you from the immoral woman, from the smooth tongue of a promiscuous woman, don't lust for her beauty... don't let her coy glances seduce you, for a prostitute will bring you to poverty, but sleeping with another man's wife will cost you your life". I remember being in a hotel room with a married woman and the husband showed up. Have you ever had an out of body experience? Well I sure did at that moment and I will break it down to you more in Volume 6, "The Man Book", along with what I call The Boaz Effect, but for now, I focus on Ruth and Naomi.

Ruth is the daughter-in-law of Naomi. They both lost their husbands, and Naomi gave Ruth permission to return to her homeland (as was customary in those days). Ruth was in a perilous position. She was in a foreign land, a widow, and very poor. Since she had no husband, she had no security, as in the Bible days the key to a woman's security was her family, or husband. However, she was committed to taking care of her mother-in-law. Naomi realized that Ruth's advantages were going to also be hers. She wasn't foolish – she wanted a good outcome for them both.

Since Naomi was the maternal figure, Ruth was willing to do any physical labor needed, however, she understood that she must depend on the wisdom of Naomi to survive. Naomi devised a plan for Ruth to execute. She anticipated that there would be a party to celebrate harvest time because this was the custom in agricultural communities. She figured that Boaz, a distant family member (in biblical times, incest was normal), would be in attendance and more than likely have a drink.

So, her advice to Ruth was, "Wait until his wits are least about him. Look as good as you can. Wash yourself and anoint yourself [that is, put on an alluring fragrance]. Put on your most attractive clothing and snuggle up to his feet at a time when he'll least expect it. Then wait and see what happens."

Ruth was not given any particular words to say. The thought was that Boaz would simply get a whiff of her fragrance, or maybe even get a glimpse of her physical beauty. Naomi's advice was focused on alluring the man. Her intention was not for Ruth to seduce Boaz on the threshing floor; Ruth would have never agreed to such a plan. But what she did desire was for the night to possess enough sexual tension so that Boaz would feel obligated to decide their future based on the power of romantic possibilities. Naomi apparently knew how all this was supposed to work...and it worked like a charm.

The Investment Effect

The investment world can be a game of cat and mouse. Those who don't understand it tend to stay away, while those who do partake in the risks. To understand how investing works, you must understand the mindset. Investing is not about today, it's about tomorrow. There is a level of pleasure and joy many people find in the process because they know that what they are doing today will pay off tomorrow (retirement), and in some cases, will reap residual income.

Dating is like the Stock Exchanges in the financial world. The New York Stock Exchange (NYSE) and the NASDAQ are Market Places where top companies and buyers connect to exchange securities ("equities and debts"). Dating websites, your job, church, restaurants, airplanes, etc. work the same way in a sense. Whereas you should have knowledge about the Stocks you buy on the New York Stock Exchange, sometimes you buy based on what you heard (stock tip). Likewise, men choose Girl A, B, C or D by what they have observed or by what they heard from a trusted friend.

Just as Boaz invested in Ruth, whether for their betterment or detriment, men invest in women. She becomes his equity or his debt; in some twisted scenarios, she may be traded for better stock. Girl B could reap him quarterly dividends while Girl C could be his capital gain.

Because many women don't understand how men think, I figured this would be an effective analogy. In investing, it's about "The Buy", "The Sell" and "The Hold"; with men there's no difference. He buys Girl B as she is either a gold digger, or he feels the need to impress her with his material goods. He sells Girl A & D because the satisfaction they offer is only temporary. However, he holds Girl C. Why? He understands her value. He knows that she will be even more priceless years from now.

I was on a popular radio show in Chicago called "Unique Perspective Love Talk Radio with Charles Dixon" and the show's title was "The Saga of Why He's with Me but Won't Marry Me". He and his guests, Rhonda Jordan-Pamon and Natalie Birdsong went into a discussion about a different type of investment – buying homes and renting apartments, and its correlation to relationships.

Rhonda said, "You should not want to rent or have a woman on loan, because you eventually want ownership. When you own something, you take better care of it".

Charles replied, "They [men] rent because they're not ready to buy. In some cases, it's an option (Rent to Own). If you could pay less to rent, would you buy?"

Natalie Birdsong replied, "There is no equity when you rent".

I found this banter between the guests and the host intriguing and thought it would be conducive to add here. I remember living in apartments, I sometimes lived out my lease and left the place without cleaning it or making repairs...I would just abandon it. However, when I moved into a home, my mentality changed.

It's the same concept with insurance – Term life is only good after I die, and that's only if the term doesn't run out first because then it benefits someone else. Whole Life, on the other hand, builds up equity and I don't have to die to enjoy it. For years I didn't own a car, I rented. Whenever I rented a car, I noticed that I never really asked about its maintenance, nor did I worry about people scratching it or running into it because my credit card insured it. I also noticed how fast I drove; how hard I would accelerate on the gas whenever the light turned green. I didn't vacuum nor did I wash the car before returning it. I eventually decided to purchase a used car and spent weeks shopping for the one that fit me.

I price bargained, paid down debt to raise my credit score, even asked the salesperson dozens of questions about that car – I especially wanted to know about the previous owner. While on the car lot I checked the mileage, popped the hood, checked the oil, radiator, brake and transmission fluid levels (on a cold engine); I even kicked the tires (I never understood why granddaddy did that).

I drove it off the lot and did the speed limit. I accelerated very gently at the green light, made sure others were looking as I pulled up to the house. I gently closed the door while exiting and as I approached my house, I turned to look at her. I unlocked the door, went inside, walked to the nearest window and took a peak at her through the curtain. I went to bed that night and heard a door slamming outside, got up and, well, you already know what I did. This routine went on for days. Why? Because I made an investment, I owned her; she was officially mine.

That said though, like automobiles, relationships can also depreciate over time. The same way I valued my car when I bought it, as it gave me problems, I started to resent having it. This is a direct correlation to the structure of the book. When a man encounters a woman he desires, the qualities he likes appear first. Only when he spends time within that relationship will he see any issues. At that point, he will be forced to determine whether the relationship is worth further investment.

The Resolve

The purpose of this book was to show you yourself through the eyes of a man to help you understand how you may be able to improve your relationship, if you so desire. Although I warned against it, I'm sure you have diagnosed yourself as either Girl A, B, C or D. You may have also found that the profile of each girl had some negative attributes that may drive the man to leave. So, what can you do to prevent this? What is the resolve? Become his everything, or what I refer to as Girl C7.

The Shulamite woman is the ideal Girl C7, as she is perfect in every way. She's the glory of the Temple of Solomon; she is the Garden of Eden; she is the Promised Land; and Solomon is absolutely smitten by her. She knows how to tap-in to Solomon by using descriptive or picture language, allegories that cause men's chests to grow. She understands that the way to a man's heart is not through his stomach (food), but through his chest (ego). The Shulamite woman describes Solomon's strengths and he describes her beauty, for they both know how to tap-in to each other's love language.

If I walk up to a woman and tell her how lovely her breasts are, I would probably be reported for sexual harassment. However, if she and I had been dating for a time and falling in love, I could say the exact same thing and it would cause her to blush. Why? Relationship.

The Song of Songs begins by saying, "This is Solomon's song of songs, more wonderful than any other" (NLT), and then this young woman says, "Kiss me and kiss me again", her king's fragrance is twice good (in Hebrew). She talks about how great his name is and she admires the fact that other women are attracted to him, surely this is working on his psyche. Sound familiar? Sure, it does, it worked back then, and it still works today.

When Solomon finally responds, he had to stop mid-sentence to say, "O most beautiful woman". Men are moved through what they see, and they must say something about it. I always say that there's a little boy in all men and the cunning women know how to tap-in to Junior. Children will always tell you the truth about yourself because they have no filter. She got his attention, spoke to his chest and became his tunnel vision, which caused him to find terms of endearments.

He became drunk with "compare-itis", found the most admired and revered objects in the Kingdom and surrounding territories to compare her to (Pharoah's stallions). The DeBeers Company coined the phrase, "Diamonds are a girl's best friend". It was an ingenious promotion; it made millions by causing both men and women to anchor diamonds with love and marriage. Yet, this is not new. Solomon said that her neck was enhanced by a string of jewels and that he was going to make her some earrings made of gold and beads of silver.

In Tyler Perry's movie, Temptation: Confession of a Marriage Counselor, Judith (Jurnee Smollett-Bell) was fed up by her husband Brice (Lance Gross) because he was boring. He kept forgetting her birthday and whenever he wanted sex, he just flat out said, "Let's have sex". Then there was Harley (Robbie Jones), a charismatic social media inventor who showed his interest by telling her things about her facial expressions that was noticeable and yet charming to him. It moved her because these were the things her own husband didn't say to her.

As the first chapter of Song of Songs concludes, Solomon does the thing men always do...he went back to the eyes. I often tell couples that men are fascinated with a woman's eyes, and the women who know this spend precious time beautifying them with color contacts and groomed lashes and brows. Notice what Solomon says in verse 15, "How beautiful you are, my darling, how beautiful! Your eyes are like doves."

There was a study on the effects of pornography on men. It was noted that men look at a woman's eyes longer than any other part of her body. The women of the night used their eyes to lure their bait. Solomon said something that sealed the deal with her; he wined and dined, did the mating call/dance and won her attention so now when she spoke, she was almost left speechless.

The Shulamite woman responds in the way a woman who is a nurturer and builder would respond – she wanted him to herself for the long haul. She said, "You are so handsome, my love, pleasing beyond words! The soft grass is our bed; fragrant cedar branches are the beams of our house, and pleasant-smelling fruit are the rafters". Yeah, he got her because you don't talk like this to a man on the first date.

Later in this romantic book, you see them touching and embracing before marriage, however, there was no intercourse. Although these two were quite expressive about their physical desires for one another, she gave a charge, four times with variations, by saying "Not to awaken love until the time is right" (vs 2:7; 3:5; 5:8; 8:4); that this unauthorized love should not be stirred up too soon. True love comes with self-control and abstinence, and once Girl C7 relays this message through her words and actions, a good man who falls in love with her will remain patient.

She already expressed to him all that she wants; she painted a good picture in his mind. Now, he's willing to move heaven and earth to taste her royal dainties someday. Men are depicted as being wild and should have the right to roam free, giving in to their created nature, which is beautifully brought out in the comparable phrase, "by the gazelles and wild deer" (vs 2:7). These animals, as majestic as they are, were never meant to be tamed; they belong in the wild, free to explore. Once the marriage bed is prepared, and the vows are made, its supper time – open the gates and call for her lion, tiger or bear, "Oh My"!

These last words from The Shulamite woman shouldn't leave anything to your imagination whatsoever, "Awake, north wind! Rise up, south wind! Blow on my garden and spread its fragrance all around. Come into your garden, my love; taste its finest fruits" (4:16).

Girl C7 was groomed from birth to exemplify the Fruit of the Spirit. She's genuine, organic and pure, to her, all things are pure (Titus 1:15). She never tries to emulate other women; they envy her.

When I was married, I remember being on my laptop and some old porn videos popped up that I forgot was there. I had lost my interest in porn by this time and while trying to clean out my system I fell asleep with the video on pause. I was awakened by my wife and boy did she let me have it! I assured her that I was only cleaning out my old life and that porn didn't excite me anymore.

One night during sex, my wife turned into a porn star. She was saying things I never heard her say and she wanted to try moves I knew she didn't like. Because it wasn't natural to me, I was turned off by it and couldn't perform. It occurred to me that my sweet wife was trying to give me the pleasure she thought I was getting by watching porn. She didn't want to lose me to a woman I would never meet. What she failed to realize though was that I wasn't into "Role Playing". Roles are temporary; eventually you are going to have to put back on your street clothes and put your toys away. Knowing this was a sensitive matter, I explained to her that I just simply wanted my wife back. I didn't require all that hard-core stuff.

When a man wants you to be somebody else, you are not his C7. The "lady in the streets and the freak in the sheets" never really dies; it doesn't always need priming, pumping and prepping. C7 rocks his world before he even asks. She makes puckered lips sounds and he wags his tail; she says heel and he sits while panting; she rubs his head and he's out like a light. Sure, he's still the head of the house, but she's the neck that turns it. He enjoys being toyed with in this manner; he feels you are paying attention to him (the little boy effect).

Why do you think men come up with sayings like, "I'll lasso the moon for you"? One episode of All in the Family entitled, "Black is the Color of My True Love's Wig", Gloria (Sally Struthers) comes home from work with a dark wig on and it excited her husband Mike "Meathead" Stivic (Rob Reiner). He couldn't keep his hands off her until she took the wig off. When they went to bed, he asked if she would put the wig back on and it finally occurred to her this wig made Mike feel like he was with another woman. She was turned off by this. Sure, I believe that a woman should change her look every now and then to spice up the relationship, but if you don't, are you still attractive to him? If the answer is no, you're not his C7.

Girl C7 is comparable to the Proverbs 31 Woman. This woman is priceless, and her husband has put his trust in her for she greatly enriches his life. This woman, like Girl C, means him only good and she will remain faithful to him for the rest of her life. She gets up early, before the break of dawn and makes breakfast for the entire house.

What many fail to see in this story is that this woman is a business owner, entrepreneur or the co-owner of a lot of land or large house (she has girls working for her). She's a great negotiator, a wise investor, and she's into real-estate. She works all night long (vs 16). She's not lazy; she works harder than anybody, but unlike these wealthy politicians of today, she gives to the poor and is very sensitive to their needs (vs 20). She's like the ant in Proverbs 6 who gathers during the summer to prepare for the winter. She ensures that everybody in her house has winter coats and warm beds.

This woman is a seamstress and apparently, she is a classy lady who knows how to paint the town red, well, "Purple" (vs 22), a mixture of red and blue associated with the rich and royalty. This virtuous woman's husband is well known in the center of town (City Hall); or maybe a philanthropist just like her and people really admire him partly because of her. He sits among civic leaders in the counsel and whenever they complement him, he turns their attention to his wife, Mrs. C7.

She is a visionary who never worries about recessions, depressions, or stock market crashes, for she's always many steps ahead of the game. She never wastes words. Whenever she speaks, it's like that old EF Hutton commercial – "When EF Hutton talks, people listen". She has the Fruit of the Spirit and she is good at taking inventory around the house to make sure they never run out of anything (vs 27).

Whenever this woman walks in a room, her children stand to acknowledge her, and her husband praises her. C7 not only loves her husband, but first and foremost, she fears the Lord and her lifestyle reflects that fact.

Out of ALL the women men desire (Girls A-D), there is only one who surpasses them all – Girl C7. These other women try to use charm, which can be deceptive. Others spend a lot of time in the mirror putting on products to impress, which don't last. Girl A, B and D are likened unto those women in the days of Noah...temporary and superficial.

The man who loves Girl C7 will literally give up his life for her, as Christ gave his life for the church (Ephesians 5:25); she is his eternal life. Notice how in the movies or in real life unfaithful men will leave their C7 to go play with others. If I had creative license over the Prodigal Son parable, I'd say he went chasing after Girl A, B and D and lost everything to them. He found himself running BACK to Girl C7 because he realized he already had everything he needed, and she willingly took him back.

Girl C7 has the playful sexual satisfaction of Girl A. She's the greener grass on the other side of the fence and arm candy of Girl B. She's the keeper of the castle, nurturer of his children, balancer of the budget and kisser of all wounds of Girl C. She's the exotic fantasy and risk taker of Girl D. Girl C7 is his multi-vitamin, yet she's not just his supplement. She is his appetizer, main course and dessert.

Epilogue

Volume 1 of Men's Chronicles: A Woman's Guide to Men, has been filled with information geared to help women understand a man's perception. It combined real life experiences as well as everyday examples from movies, music, television and books, to provide insight into the male psyche.

In the subsequent volumes, 2-5, we will delve more into the mindset of these individual women. We will explore their behaviors, thought patterns and beliefs to determine whether it is possible, or even necessary to pursue a different lifestyle to obtain true love. Although I named the four women, the truth is that it doesn't simply describe one woman. Like the Proverbs 31 Woman, these ladies represent a variety of women that happen to possess similar attributes.

You will meet Lola, the Lady of Sorrow, in Volume 2. This is a lady who loves a man with all that she has but may never be his first choice. Unfortunately, she is only looked at as his sex toy, his fantasy, his freak.

Bella (Beautiful) is introduced in the next volume. This woman is eye candy for most men; she is who they desire but may never be able to obtain. They continue to chase her because they love the challenge.

In Volume 4, you will encounter Phoebe, who is shining and pure. She is his heart, his lifeline. She is the one for whom he would lay down his life. But unfortunately, she is also the one whom he takes advantage of and almost loses.

Finally, Lilleth, of the night, appears in Volume 5. She is a woman who, as her name suggests has a dark personality. She battles various issues (mental, emotional, and sexual), yet is very appealing to him.

Let me answer the question before you ask...no, I am not writing a follow-up book called, The Four Men that Women Desire to address Volume 1. However, Volume 6, The Ultimate Man Book will expound more on the various types of men that exist. It will discuss their qualities and characteristics in detail to help determine whether they should be desired as a life partner within the confines of a relationship.

Finally, we will conclude this series with Volume 7, and address The Psychology of Sex. For many men, sex is the driving factor for how they choose their women. But in this book, I am going to delve into the seven factors that affect his perspective toward this topic.

As previously stated, my goal in writing this series is not simply to share my beliefs on love. My desire is to provide you with enough information on the subject so that you can make better choices for yourself and stop living with regret.

Made in the USA
San Bernardino, CA
15 June 2020